A PRACTICAL GUIDE TO

PHOTOGRAPHIC INTELLIGENCE

HAROLD HOUGH

Loompanics Unlimited
Port Townsend, Washington

A PRACTICAL GUIDE TO
PHOTOGRAPHIC INTELLIGENCE
© 1990 by Harold Hough
Printed in USA

Published by:
Loompanics Unlimited
PO Box 1197
Port Townsend, WA 98368

Photo Credits:

Cover photo by Harold Hough

Figures 1-1, 1-2, 1-4, and 1-5 by Harold Hough

All other photographs are public domain

Illustrations by Shellay Maughan

ISBN 1-55950-053-0
Library of Congress
  Catalog Card Number 90-063309

Contents

Dedicated To

Ken Trbovich
Proof that Renaissance men still exist.

Introduction

The Stealth Bomber was shown to the media in 1988 and some of America's most jealously guarded secrets were available for the price of a camera. *Aviation Week* went further than the others and hired a plane to fly over the B2 bomber in order to photograph the wing configuration. The photos revealed the over-the-wing exhausts and moving flaps that are responsible for reducing the infrared signature. Others, less adventurous, used telephoto lenses to photograph aircraft characteristics that revealed much to an aerospace engineer. The large cockpit windows indicated that the crew was set back from the windows. This was confirmed by comparing photos of the ejection seat hatches. Photos of the wing angles and the inlet designs were enough to give experts an idea of flight characteristics and speed. Even the shading of the different parts of the aircraft revealed the radar location, where the radar absorbing material was applied, and where maintenance hatches were.

Photographic intelligence is just as useful in a closed society like the USSR. Photos taken by Thomas Cochran of the Natural Resources Defense Council, during a visit to a test center, revealed a laser director that can direct a ruby or carbon dioxide laser at aircraft or satellite targets. At the Paris Air Show, photos of a Su-27 showed that it was designed for rough field operations because of its landing gear design and the protective gear in the engine air inlets.

These examples prove that photographic intelligence isn't the exclusive domain of spy satellites, superspies, and exotic equipment. Valuable photos can be produced with an average camera and an intelligent operator, even under the eyes of the most paranoid counter-espionage group.

Nor is photographic intelligence just the playground of the superpowers or even the military. This book can help a business legally discover the competition's activities, a journalist investigate a story, a private investigator on a case, a business copy documents without paying unreasonable rates for microfilming, and make the amateur a better photographer.

This book also has some value for those who are trying to hide something. Security officers, after reading this book, will have a better idea of what someone can learn about classified matters, even without entering the premises. But, most important, the average reader will find out how much the government can legally learn from observing you and your actions.

The Fourth Amendment of the U.S. Constitution protects our "persons, houses, papers, and effects against unreasonable searches and seizures." However, the courts have diluted this in order to allow the authorities to use several high-tech surveillance methods, including photography, to invade your privacy. Aerial photography is often used by the government for everything from tax assessment to drug searches. And long-range photography can peer into your house and reveal much that you would prefer to remain secret (with computer enhancement, even the text of documents). Since the courts have ruled that this isn't unreasonable search, it's up to us be aware of this threat.

Although photographic intelligence can threaten our freedom, it can also protect it. We often associate intelligence with governments, but it can be used against them. Outside of the obvious uses in guerrilla warfare, we can use photographic intelligence in peacetime to cut away the veil of secrecy that crooked politicians and bureaucrats use to hide their actions. Although this book deals with military subjects, the same techniques can be used to track the civilian sectors of government.

So, whether you are a businessman, policeman, student, member of the military, civil libertarian, or some other sort of reader, this book offers something to interest you. May it be entertaining, educational, and thought provoking.

1

Basics of
Photographic Intelligence

For those of you who can't wait until the end of the book to use the principles of photographic intelligence, I will provide a quick overview of its basics.

The most important thing to remember is that a good photo must be supported with good data. A sharp photo taken at high risk, of a special component of the Stealth fighter, is worthless unless it is identified as belonging to the F-117A. A good photo must be accompanied by at least the following data:

- Exact location
- Exact measurement
- Orientation
- Time and date
- Explanation of why the object is important

The next most significant point is to bring out the feature that has the most importance. In other words, if the bridge you are photographing has a platoon of tanks guarding it, make sure the tanks are in the photo. Imagine the embarrassment of the lightly armed paratroopers who may be asked to take the objective.

If possible, take a set of three photographs. The distant shot sets the target in a location. The medium shot and a close up will show detail.

Include landmarks in location shots. This orients the viewer and may provide some evidence of the target's use.

Remember that a photographer who's captured hasn't accomplished anything. If taking a photograph creates suspicion, carefully weigh the need for the photo. For instance, if a picture can be taken at a distance, without detail or causing any problems, take it and turn it in. A skilled analyst can learn much from a long-distance photo (some of this will be covered in the chapter on interpretation). If necessary, another mission (with proper support) can be launched to gain other information.

Film is cheap. If you see something interesting, photograph it. Many intelligence coups are the result of extra work. Even if it doesn't have current use, it may be important in the future. In the 1930's, no one thought that tourist photos of Europe would be used in WW II. Nor did tourists to Grenada realize that some of their photos would be used to plan the U.S. invasion in 1983.

Some Examples

The following photos have intelligence value. (See Figures 1-1 through 1-8.) The captions explain why these shots are of interest.

Figure 1-1

A tourist photo like this one has some military value.

Figure 1-2

Without the preceding photo (Figure 1-1), this detail shot is cryptic.

Figure 1-3

Be aware of unusual buildings. This one is a wind tunnel.

Figure 1-4

Be alert for any photo opportunity. Although this photo is fuzzy, it shows a German fighter outside of Germany. Such information can help determine deployment.

Figure 1-5

*Follow-up chance photos. After shooting the fighter in Figure 1-4, I photographed
the whole base. This shot was taken from on top of my vehicle.*

Figure 1-6

This photo shows a concealed World War II Japanese gun emplacement.

Figure 1-7

This photo shows where the gun emplacement in Figure 1-6 is concealed.

Figure 1-8

The arrow in this photo indicates where the gun emplacement in Figure 1-6 is placed on the hill.

2

Equipment

A quarter of a century of James Bond movies has spoiled us. We think photographic intelligence requires super-sophisticated equipment in order to provide worthwhile information.

Probably the most realistic camera seen in a James Bond film was in the opening credits of *License to Kill,* an Olympus OM-4. Although sophisticated and expensive, it was on the right track. The best camera for photographic intelligence is the 35mm single lens reflex camera (SLR). They are small, easy to carry, have many accessories, use common film (have you tried to buy film for a Hasselblad in a grocery store in Barcelona?), have the largest number of film types available, are easy to use, inconspicuous (try to position a view camera in front of a foreign military establishment), and best of all, they are cheap. Unless you are on a government payroll with unlimited expenses, just stay with a 35mm SLR. If you are with a government agency and have an unlimited expense account, remember it's the person behind the camera, not the camera, that makes a good photograph. Poorly spent taxpayer dollars will not make you a better photographer.

Camera Body

I will not spend time discussing the best camera body. If you need more information, I suggest a basic photography book. Chances are you already have a body good enough for photographic intelligence (camera body, that is). However, I will address a couple of issues to consider if you are going to buy your first SLR.

Aside from cost, the major consideration is the type of accessories available for your camera. Unless you have a cheap camera, you probably have a wide selection of equipment to support your work. A major name camera like Minolta, Nikon, Olympus, Pentax, etc., will have all the accessories you need. They are also popular enough that you can buy a lens at most stores in the U.S., if you suddenly need one.

If you have not selected a camera, it may be important to decide which type you want. Most systems have been around for a few years and have bodies ranging from mechanical to "super gee whiz" electronic. While the electronics offer convenience, just don't get caught with a dead battery. Then all you have is an expensive paper weight. On the other hand, the older mechanical cameras require more thought, but can operate if the battery dies. I was once thirty feet underground, in the arctic tundra, in thirty below zero temperatures, 250 miles from the nearest camera store, with an electronic camera and a dead battery. As soon as I returned to civilization, I bought a mechanical one. Enough said.

If you have enough money, both an electronic camera body and a mechanical one are recommended. You always have a backup in an emergency and you still have the electronics if you need to take that snapshot of the Stealth fighter buzzing overhead.

Lenses

A cheap camera and an expensive lens is better than an expensive body and a cheap lens. If you are going to spend some money, spend it on lenses. A body is just a light box. If the shutter is accurate (and most are), the rest of the doodads on a camera body can be replaced by a human brain. On the other hand, the lens gathers and focuses the light. A good lens can gather more light and focus it more sharply than a cheap one. A good lens can be the difference between a sharp hand-held photo and a murky shot taken with a tripod.

Using these considerations as a guide, let's look at the needs for photographic intelligence. Again, if you need to know more about lenses, please read a basic book about photography.

Your lens choice will be based on the type of photographic intelligence you will be involved in. However, I will examine a few of the options and some choices to be made. Remember that lenses are a series of compromises between speed, sharpness, weight, and money. You will have to make the final decisions.

The most basic choice to be made concerns the focal length of the lens. Most cameras come with the 50mm, but chances are this isn't what you need. If you are buying a camera, avoid the 50mm and find a better choice. The type to buy depends on the type of photography. Although a telephoto seems the obvious choice for photographic intelligence, that may very well not be true. A telephoto can provide detail of a distant installation, but it can't include landmarks and surrounding terrain, like a wide angle lens can.

An obvious choice is a zoom lens. These can cover several critical focal lengths in one convenient package. They are easier to handle, less obvious, and cheaper than buying several fixed focal length lenses.

The question of what type of zoom lens to choose is harder to answer. I have seen ones that cover everything from 28mm to 210mm. However, such a broad number of focal lengths means the manufacturer had to sacrifice speed and sharpness (more about those later). I suggest you have two zoom lenses (one for each of the two camera bodies you have). One can go from wide angle to mild telephoto (ex. 28mm — 100mm), while the other goes from where the other one stops to about 200mm. These should meet most of your needs, and if you have two cameras, will allow you to shoot without changing lenses.

Although these two lenses will cover most situations, there may be a need for a longer telephoto. Here there are two different types of lens. While you can still buy the standard telephoto, there is a mirror lens, which gives you a long focal length lens in a much shorter size. Although less conspicuous than a traditional telephoto, they also have less versatility and resolution than the others.

For the person who needs a much longer lens and is good with his hands, there is the compound refractive lens. This type of lens uses a long focus lens and a couple of mirrors to reflect the image back and forth to the film plane. Instructions for the construction of this device can be found in *Applied Surveillance Photography*, by Raymond Siljander.

So far we've talked about lenses without discussing the trade-offs. The first is sharpness. Obviously, the more complex the lens, the more glass is in it. Although the glass is high quality, the more of it you have between the object and the film, the less detail and sharpness you will have. Consequently, zoom lenses will lack the sharpness of a fixed length lens.

Although zoom lenses lack sharpness, many question its importance. Most commercial lenses are sharp enough that the average person looking at the average snapshot will not notice the difference. Therefore, many times greater sharpness isn't important. For instance, if you are using a fast film, which has less resolution, a sharp lens isn't going to help. On the other hand, if you are using a high resolution film and you need the detail, sharpness counts. Although many lens manufacturers claim to make quality lenses, one maker with a good reputation, whose lenses can be used on most 35mm cameras, is Tokina.

Speed costs. A 200mm telephoto can be bought for a couple hundred dollars. A similar one with an f stop of 2 could easily run $5,000. A 210mm lens that has an f stop of 1.2 costs over $40,000! The moral? Speed is important, but don't pay for any more than you need. The reason: a fast lens requires more light, which means more ground glass to gather the light and focus it properly. Of course, more glass means sharpness suffers. In addition, faster lenses mean more critical focusing. It makes sense for you to use faster film rather than spend a fortune for a super-fast lens.

Don't let the previous discourse mislead you. Speed *is* important. That's why the mirror lenses are at a disadvantage. They only have one f-stop, which means you need fast film or a bright day. Again, let the situation be your guide.

The final consideration in your lens purchase is cost. A good rule of thumb is that the more a lens costs, the better it is. Again, you have to consider your situation. If you can live with some trade-offs, you can cut your cost down. For instance, if you need a long telephoto, like 1000 to 4000mm, it might make sense to buy a telescope and a camera adaptor. They will be very slow and the sharpness will leave something to be desired, but you can buy some impressive capability for under $100. Just don't expect to sell the photos to *National Geographic*.

This was a brief overview of lenses. If you need more information, the best place to go is your local camera shop or the book store for a book on lenses. They can provide you with technical information for the beginner.

Accessories

The 35mm SLR camera is the Barbie doll of the photographic world. No one is satisfied with the basic kit. You need to buy more and more accessories. There are several extras that are necessary for photographic intelligence. They are:

- Photographer's Bag — To store all the stuff you are going to buy.

- Tripod — A necessity for low light or telephoto shots. Since they are conspicuous, buy a "quick set up" type.

- Mini Tripod — Since the large tripods are too noticeable, a mini tripod or a bean bag can provide a steady shot without raising eyebrows.

- Cable release — A must for tripod shots.

- Tele-extender — These can increase the focal length of a telephoto lens without the cost or inconvenience of carrying another lens.

- Polaroid filter — You can decrease glare in your photos.

- Extra batteries — They always give out at the worst time.

- Notebook — Take notes of all your shots.

- Compass — For providing directions.

- Swiss Army Knife — Buy the best one you can. It will definitely come in handy.

Obviously this can't cover everything needed. Much of what you need will be determined by the specific mission. Start with these, and as you plan your shots (next chapter), you will start to discover other needs.

3

Planning
The Photograph

Before you start a photographic intelligence trip, know what subjects you may encounter. Using a map, trace the exact route you will take and note any bridges, dams, cities, military installations, or factories that you will pass. Even if you aren't on a military mission, just a commercial operation to photograph a competitor's factory, other photos may be important to analyzing the target. For instance, transportation facilities may provide the analyst with an idea of the type and amount of materials that are shipped.

Using all the available information you can gather on each target, determine what features need to be photographed, the best angle, and what view may have the least obstructions. Analyze the subject. What is it? Where is it? How big is it? How many shots are needed to cover the subject? What type of views would be best for it? The answers will help you determine the equipment you need and any additional information you must have.

An intelligent photographer can help the mission by knowing the subject. That should include reading about the subject in an encyclopedia or other book and then speaking with an expert. By reading about the subject, the photographer becomes familiar enough with the basics to take useful pictures and recognize anything out of the ordinary that should be the subject of additional shots.

Once you finish the reading, speak with an expert familiar with the mission who can fill you in on the latest developments, special photographic requirements, and certain items or activities that may indicate unusual activities. Obviously the specialist should be cleared for details on the mission and, if possible, should be the same one who will interpret the photos. This allows him to tell you what he is looking for, any special requirements that he may have, and any suggestions specific to the target you will be visiting. When you read the chapters on resolution and photographic interpretation, you will learn how the interpreter can help define the needs of the mission.

Studying the target and its technologies can't be overemphasized. It only takes a couple of days, can be done where the risk of discovery is low, makes the photographer better able to identify additional targets at the site, and limits risk because a knowledgeable photographer is faster and less likely to be caught.

After reaching the target and pinpointing the subject, take a good clear photograph as soon as possible. That prevents the mission from being a total failure if you attract attention or are forced to leave the area. After taking this photo, you can concentrate on taking the best shot from the best view. If the best view is unavailable, settle for the second best.

Your series of exposures should include landmarks, or recognizable parts of town. The best option is to shoot a panorama. Sweep the camera through a set of overlapping shots that includes the target in the center shot. This allows the interpreter to identify the location and includes other items at the site that may be of interest to the expert. A couple of 360 degree panoramas of the same area can give the interpreter enough information to correlate bearings, determine distances, verify information from a map, or add detail to an aerial photograph.

After shooting, the photographer should make a sketch of the installation and note directions, any distances, and where each shot was taken. Then he should note any important parts of the target, and determine where the best view of that part is available.

A good set of photos should cover the target from 360 degrees, should have medium and close-up shots of key items, and should have markers that help the interpreter determine distances in the shot. Remember, good photographic intelligence is a result of planning, knowledge, and opportunity.

In addition to your own sketches, obtain local maps and overlay your shooting positions on it. This may give you some additional details to shoot or note in your report, add some critical distances to your sketch, and may allow you to note any mistakes or obvious errors in the preprinted map. Sometimes a country like the USSR will tamper with the information on maps to mislead the opposition. Your on-the-site observations can uncover such tampering and may lead others to ask why the opposition wants to mislead you.

The preceding discussion assumes everything works properly. It never does. The target may be obstructed by trees or fences. If it is obstructed, move to a hill or climb on top of your vehicle for a better shot (that's why motor homes are good travel vehicles).

If the target is too far away, a photograph with a long telephoto lens may be the only solution. Before tackling the long shots, get the location shots to allow the interpreter to place it. Then use your longest telephoto and any extenders you have. Since heat can cause distortions of extremely long shots, you should take your shot in the early morning, while the ground is still cool. You should pay attention to haze, and have a solid tripod to take a steady photo. If there is too much haze, an infrared film may help. Otherwise, you should use the finest grain film you can use. The chapters on resolution and film will have additional information on obtaining the highest resolution photographs.

Although 360 degree panoramas are the best area shots, they may not be possible. In that case, the photographer should take a partial panorama with a couple of landmarks (if that is impossible, use the compass to note the direction of the panorama). Then move to another site and take another partial panorama, including the landmarks or noting the direction. This allows the interpreter to plot your position.

Another panorama can be taken from a moving car, train, airplane, or ship. You merely take a series of shots as you move along. The photos should overlap, and if possible, should overlap by 60 percent (that is, picture 2 includes at least 60% of what's in picture 1). That way, a stereo view can be made. Be sure to note the speed of the vehicle and the time or distance between photographs.

Stereo views are excellent for showing distances, and helping identify individual features and detail. If the target is relatively close, they are made by taking two photos from positions three to four inches apart. As the distance to the target increases, however, you increase the distance between the two camera positions to help in identifying distance. Here are the instructions for taking stereo photographs:

1. Take the first shot.

2. If the target is no further than 100 yards, move the camera 2.5 inches to the left or right from the first position and take the second shot.

3. As the target distance increases, the distance between the two camera positions should increase by a ratio of 1:100. If the subject is 1000 yards away, the camera positions should be about 10 yards apart.

4. Except for moving the camera to the left or right, the optical axis shouldn't change for either shot.

5. The foreground should be kept clear.

Again, a good book on photography should provide some clues on taking good photos. However, here are some recommendations that pertain to photographic intelligence:

- You know what you are looking at. Draw attention to it in the photo by centering it. The interpreter may not know what you are photographing.

- Make the set of shots tell a story. Give general appearance, relationship to terrain and other objects, size, shape, and construction. Take several shots from all points of the compass. Provide wide angle shots, panoramas, close-ups of important features, and medium shots to relate features to each other.

- Show detail. Construction methods, materials and equipment may provide additional information.

- Keep equipment, especially lenses, clean.

- If in doubt, overexpose print film and underexpose slide film.

- Don't get artistic. Conventional positions with proper exposure will provide the best information.

- If things aren't perfect, take a shot now and come back later, if possible.

- Show the horizon. This helps the interpreter place the shot. If the horizon is impossible to shoot, include a man-made item like a road that can help someone reconstruct the horizon.

- Always include an item that has a known size so the interpreter can determine the size of other items in the photo. If you can't include a ruler, then cars, equipment, and people, can give an idea of size.

- Be critical of your own work. When you receive the prints, ask yourself if they convey the information you tried to obtain.

- Annotate copies of the photographs to bring attention to features you feel should be emphasized.

- Relate the target to the surrounding area. Note where roads, rails, and power lines are in the photo or in the surrounding area.

- Practice with your gear in off hours. Don't put it away after a mission. You can experiment during your spare time, become more familiar with the equipment, and learn how to improve on previous blunders. This practice also has a couple of side benefits. The first is that you may come upon a target of opportunity that should be shot and studied. The second is that you will get a reputation as a camera bug and will attract less attention when you carry photographic equipment on a mission.

4

Photographing Military Targets

It's impossible to list all the military targets that a photographer should be aware of. This chapter lists key activities, the type of features to be photographed, and the type of photography best for the subject. Remember that the technical quality of the photo is just as important as the target.

Aviation Activity

Sites

The photographer should look for air bases, landing fields, level strips that could be used by gliders or light aircraft, seaplane bases, landing, dispersal, and taxi areas, runways, mats, decks, catapults, arresting gear, and other landing and take-off equipment.

Show the overall appearance: landmarks, surroundings, or related features. Shoot approaches, hazards, and obstructions for aircraft and provide measurements, sizes and shapes. Take photos of the runway surface and construction and note any special launching devices like catapults.

Use panoramas or distant shots to show over-all appearance and surroundings. Medium shots and close-ups should show construction, details of the installation, and unusual equipment.

Aircraft

The photographer should note aircraft types and onboard equipment.

The type of features you should note fall into two different categories, tactical and engineering. Tactical information would include numbers of aircraft, types, makes, stage of development, and recognition features. Engineering information would consist of power plant, landing gear, visible electronics, external equipment, wing configuration inlets and exhausts, surface controls.

The best shots of aircraft are medium shots, with close-ups of specific equipment. Photos should also be taken of aircraft in flight, landing and taking off. Front, side and rear shots can also be useful in providing identification.

Facilities

The photographer should shoot hangers, repair shops, ramps, warehouses, fueling sites, fuel storage, underground sites, firing and bombing ranges, test cells, and wind tunnels.

You should emphasize the type of structure: size, shape, and capacity. Close-up photos should note structural details like reinforcing, earthworks, and other protective features. Photos of activity can also show the use and relate it to the rest of the facility.

You should use medium shots for the buildings and close-ups of details.

Ground Support Equipment

Photograph towing equipment, trucks, crash equipment, generators, and starting equipment.

Photographs should emphasize the type of equipment and its use. Try to note size and fabrication details.

Use medium views to show equipment and activities. Close-ups can provide detail on manufacturing methods.

Electronics

Photograph power and telephone lines, microwave towers, broadcast facilities, radar equipment, the control tower, antennas, and power plants.

Photographs should note the relation of the targets to the airfield and its use. Special attention should be paid to noting size, shape, height, and arrangement of antennas and radar.

Use panoramas to show power distribution and communication lines, and medium and close-ups of facilities in order to reveal detail. Antenna photos should have the sky as a background. A cluttered background can confuse the photographic interpreters.

Defenses

Photograph anti-aircraft and rocket positions. Note guard positions, fences, check points, and other obstructions and defensive positions.

The photos should show the general arrangement of the defenses, identifying features, firepower, types of weapons, fields of fire, access to positions, and activity (like changing the guard or drills).

Use panorama shots to show general arrangement, fields of fire, and location of defensive sites. Medium and close-up shots should identify key features and show camouflage.

Naval and Maritime Activities

Ports

The photographer should shoot anchorages, piers, break-waters, oil terminals, and channels.

Shots should emphasize landmarks, general layout, size, shape, accessibility, use, development, and unusual features.

The best photos will use panoramas or distant shots and show layout and related landmarks and features. An idea of channel depth can be given by showing a ship.

Ships

Photograph all vessels.

Emphasize the type and nationality of all vessels. Show measurements, weapons, superstructure, antennas, radar, and any unusual activity.

Use medium shots for overall appearance and close-ups for pertinent details.

Facilities

Photograph basins, piers, docks, cranes, wharves, and cargo.

Highlight locations, dimensions, shapes, capacities, mobility of equipment, and structural details. Photograph all loading and unloading activities in addition to the cargo. Photos should help identify the types of cargo that can be handled at the port (bulk, containerized, oil, etc.).

Support Services

Photograph transportation facilities, railway yards, warehouses, open storage, fuel tanks, drydocks, roads, power lines, pipelines, repair shops, munitions storage, and testing sites.

Stress location, type, size, structural features, capacity, and relationship to the ships and other transportation facilities. Show the capability of transportation and shipping facilities.

Use panoramas and distant shots to show over-all view. Medium shots and close-ups to show types of buildings, equipment, and materials.

Military Bases

Installations

Photograph headquarters, posts, camps, forts, ports of embarkation, staging areas, military reservations, test sites, and maneuvers.

Photographs should show appearance, size, shape, landmarks, and characteristic features. Photos should note type of military at the site and units involved. Show the accessibility of the facility and the types of transportation available.

Panoramas and distance shots are needed to show the whole facility, relation to other landmarks, relation to towns, and approaches. Medium and close-up shots are needed to show buildings and the type of units at the site.

Defenses

Fortifications, artillery, anti-aircraft and anti-tank positions should be noted.

Photos should emphasize arrangement, size of the defenses, fields of fire, capabilities, type of weapons, and any activity like changing of the guard or drills. Special attention should be paid to relating defensive points to landmarks and showing camouflage or concealment.

Use distant or medium shots to show arrangement, dispersal, and fields of fire. Close-ups should be used to identify structures, and types and numbers of weapons.

Ordnance

Photograph weapons, vehicles, and equipment.

Shots should emphasize features, size, shape, and capability of the weapons.

Use medium shots and close-ups to show general appearance and size. Close-ups can be used to show manufacture, unit markings, and modifications.

Services

Photograph arsenals, depots, warehouses, dumps, storage areas, repair facilities, transportation facilities, proving grounds, and maneuver areas.

Photos should emphasize general appearance and identifying features. Attention should be paid to the type of material handled, how it is handled, how it is stored, and how it is moved. Repair sites should be identified as to their capability and the number of items under current repair. Also note if any modifications can or are being made with equipment. Photograph equipment at proving grounds and in maneuver areas. Attention should be paid to equipment at proving grounds, since it may have modifications. Photos should give as much information about capability as possible.

Use panoramas and distant shots to show overall relationship of facilities. Medium shots and close-ups are needed to show methods of storing, processing, or repairing.

Concealed Activity

Covered shops, storage facilities, and manufacturing sites should be photographed.

Emphasize location, access, dimensions, shape, and unique activities. Note all transportation facilities around the site and photograph any materials entering or leaving the site.

Use panoramas and distant shots to show general location. Carefully note directions so interpreters can pinpoint the location. Use medium and close-up shots to show features and activities.

Tactics

Photograph troop and equipment deployments, unit discipline, siting of weapons, active and passive defense measures. Special attention should be placed on activities, especially drills and maneuvers.

Emphasize identifying features of each activity, routes, communications, equipment placement, fields of fire, and reaction to unexpected events like weather.

Use distant shots and medium views to show activity and its relationship to the area. Close-ups should be used to show details of the equipment and activities.

Sites for Troop Insertion

General Physical Geography

Photograph coastlines, large clearings, clearings near important installations.

Photograph landmarks, general appearance, configuration of the land, vegetation, trees, buildings, type of soil, and peculiarities of the area.

Use 360-degree panoramas from a couple of sites to provide relationships of terrain and distances. Medium and close-up shots of buildings and landmarks should be taken. Close-ups of soil and vegetation are also needed.

Beaches

Photograph coastlines and water.

Emphasize visual landmarks, usable and unusable portions of the coast. Identify low-water and high-water marks on the beach. Show where the beach ends and dunes, cliffs or other terrain starts.

Use panoramas and distant views to locate ideal and marginal landing sites. Using a boat for some of this work would be ideal if it wouldn't raise suspicions. Perhaps a fishing trip would provide the best cover. Medium shots of buildings, defensive positions, and terrain are needed. A photograph of a person and a car in the sand would provide loading information.

Amphibious Sites

Photograph places where boats may pull along side man-made or natural features to disembark troops. Show sea approaches, obstructions, sea conditions.

Emphasize the relationship of landmarks to the sites. Give dimensions of sites and construction or terrain characteristics. Photograph the approaches and indicate possible depth, hazards, reefs, wrecks, and hazardous currents. Identify the location of breakwaters and buoys. Identify sea conditions by photographing the sea state, types of craft in the water, debris washed onto the beach, and construction that may identify hazardous conditions.

Photos should be panoramas or distant shots, especially from the sea. Medium shots should be made of hazards or buildings and close-ups of beach erosion or debris.

Clearings for Airborne Assaults

Photograph golf courses, parks, farms, and parking lots.

Emphasize location in relationship to landmarks visible from the air. Note all aerial obstructions like trees, power lines, and radio antennas. Photograph vegetation and its thickness and depth. Identify possible airborne approaches (through valleys, around obstacles, and away from populated areas) with photos.

Panoramas from different sites will provide distances and relationships. Aerial photographs or shots from hills would help identify the site from the air. Distant shots should identify obstacles and aerial routes. Medium and close-ups should provide detail of obstacles and vegetation.

Defenses

Photograph troop placements, artillery, anti-tank positions, anti-air positions, and buildings.

Emphasize location, number, power, field of fire, types of weapons and communications. Note troop readiness and state of defensive positions.

Panorama shots showing defensive positions and fields of fire are invaluable. Medium and close-ups of positions and equipment should also be taken.

Facilities

Photograph any potential landing site that would be of value to invading forces.

Topography of the surrounding area should be photographed. Natural exits from the area, natural obstructions like cliffs, swamps, and ridges should be noted. Roads, their size, load-bearing ability, and construction should be photographed. Other transportation facilities (rail, water, air) should be photographed with particular attention to capabilities. Bridges, powerplants, and fuel installations should also be photographed.

Distant shots and panoramas will show interrelationships of various items. Medium views of key pieces of terrain or transportation facilities are needed, as well as close-ups of road surfaces, vegetation, and some terrain (like cliffs to show ability to climb).

Basic Services

Transportation and Communications

Photograph railways, highways, water and air routes, microwave towers, phone lines, power distribution equipment, and power lines.

Photos should emphasize the relation to the area, importance to the military and economy, direction, destination, and amount of traffic.

Use panoramas or distant shots to show routes, location, and relationship to landmarks. Medium views and close-ups should be taken of equipment or to describe construction.

Installations

Photograph power stations, radio and tv stations, pumping stations, computer centers, repair and maintenance shops.

Emphasize identifying features, size, shape, structure, and use. Note relationships to military facilities or equipment.

Show the facilities with medium shots and details with close-ups.

Isolated Features

Photograph bridges, tunnels, dams, locks, reservoirs, transshipping facilities, weather stations, and observation stations.

Photos should emphasize location, and relationship to the country infrastructure. Photos of bridges, tunnels, and dams should indicate importance, size, features, and any defensive positions. Photos of bridges and tunnels should indicate load-bearing capability, width, and clearance. Attention should be also paid to footings, foundations, and structural joints.

Photos should be distant shots to show area and approaches. Medium shots and close-ups should show detail of the structure and indicate dimensions.

Equipment

Photograph railroad equipment, barges, ferries, generators, transformers, etc.

Emphasize size, shape, type and use.

Use medium shots to place equipment in a site. Use close-ups to identify features and capabilities. If the site isn't restricted, a shot of the equipment plates may be possible.

Experimental Research Facilities

Laboratories

Emphasize the relationship of the site to the surrounding area, size, shape, characteristic features, and type of activity.

Use distant shots to locate site and medium and close-up photos to highlight detail.

Test Sites

Photograph proving grounds, firing ranges, launching sites, pilot plants, installations, etc.

Emphasize location and relationship to landmarks. Note layout, defense, security measures, and activity.

Use panorama photos to show site. Medium shots can be used for smaller features like buildings.

Equipment

Photos should show features, size, and use. If the equipment is similar to a production item, photograph any differences.

Use medium photos to show appearances and close-ups to show detail, method of construction, and differences with current models.

Products

Photograph identifying features, size, shape, and characteristics. Note if it is to be used in military efforts.

Use medium shots to show handling and shipping of products. Close-ups can show details.

Culture

Cities and Towns

Photograph site, terrain, activities, and transportation.

Emphasize landmarks, approaches, and general appearance. Photograph typical industrial activity. Use 360-degree panoramas to provide location, distances, and relationships. Medium shots can detail activities.

Rural

Photograph villages, farms, agricultural facilities.

Photos should emphasize types of buildings and the nature of the economy. Photograph food processing facilities and the size of storage bins. Pay attention to structures that may have a military use or may be mistaken for a military site.

Use medium shots to show size and location. Overall capabilities of the area are more important than specific locations of facilities.

Customs

Photograph typical buildings, materials, arrangements, methods, and sizes.

Photos should show the effect of customs on the construction of buildings. Street layouts and parks should be emphasized.

Use medium shots to show character. Close-up shots can show detail of construction.

People

Photographs should show characteristics, dress, temperament, and discipline.

Emphasize the relationship of uniformed forces with the population. Note the quality of dress and identify if clothing is generally new or used. Is the society disciplined or individualistic?

Use medium and close-up candid views if possible.

Terrain and Vegetation

Nature of Terrain

Photograph natural routes of movement, obstacles to movement, and major vegetation stands.

Photos should emphasize landmarks, general topography, major valley routes, critical slopes, stream crossings, type of field boundaries, swamps, and types of structures.

Use panoramas from high points to tie in landmarks. Stereo shots are useful in this type of work. Medium shots can locate key obstacles, slopes, and natural routes.

Soil Types

Photos should show rock outcrops, and the load-bearing ability of the soil.

Emphasize the condition in critical areas. Show details of soil and rock texture.

Use medium views to show outcrops and the load ability of the soil. Close-ups can detail load-bearing ability and soil texture.

Tree Types

Photograph underbrush, grasses, swamp and marsh vegetation.

Emphasize the size, details of shape, and location of principal types of vegetation.

Use medium and close-up views of plants to show characteristics.

Government Facilities

Sites

Photograph offices and residences of the Head of State, legislative buildings, judicial buildings, police headquarters and posts, radio and television stations, the treasury, and other sites important to an opposing force.

Use distant photos to show the target in relation to landmarks. Use medium and close-up shots to show details of the building (like entrances and windows). Emphasize living quarters, possible points of resistance, escape routes, and weak points.

Procedures

Photos should show entrances and security procedures, press and public access, ease of access, number of tourists, and security in major events.

Use medium photos to show subject and close-ups to show detail. Emphasize normal procedures and anything that may indicate heightened security. The photos should emphasize the differences between normal and unusual security. Photograph any disruption of procedures to indicate the reaction of security forces.

Defenses

Photograph type and numbers of military, positions, barriers, barracks, fences, nearest reinforcements, and their route. Emphasize the type of weapons carried by the defense force.

Photographs should include distant shots to indicate defensive positions in relation to the rest of the area. Medium shots should show specific positions, while close ups should show equipment.

Support Services

Photograph facilities that have regular access to government buildings. These include: food services, janitorial services, office equipment repair, and supplies. Photograph the vehicles that enter government sites and emphasize the procedures for their access and which entrances they use.

Distant photos should place the facilities in relation to landmarks. Medium shots should show detail and access to government sites. Close-up pictures of papers or identification would be useful.

Facilities

Photograph helicopter pads, airports, signs of underground facilities, transportation facilities, microwave towers. Emphasize procedures surrounding the movement of a VIP (type of craft, direction taken, security, etc.). Also note direction and dimensions of antennas, microwave towers, and satellite dishes.

Use distant shots to place the facility in the general area. Medium and close-up photos should be used to show details and procedures.

5

Commercial Intelligence Targets

Although the following targets have military value, they may be of more importance to a competitor. Industrial intelligence, however, has different requirements. It doesn't require certain information, like exact location and landmarks, because most businesses don't plan to launch a bomber strike against their competitors (it's considered tacky). Nor are security arrangements as important, unless the competition plans an illegal break-in (the location of security can, however, indicate important locations at the site). On the other hand, industrial intelligence emphasizes manufacturing techniques and cost information.

Factories

Activity

Photograph mining, refining, machine shops, and production lines.

Stress the size of the plant, and the position and size of features that may give an idea of function or capacity (piping, stacks, towers, etc.). During working hours the photographer should shoot the parking lot and the cars. The cars will indicate how many workers are at the site and their relative salaries. Note the appearance of the workers, since the attire can give an inkling of the type of work. Photographing workers leaving before, at, and after quitting time will give an idea of work load, what jobs are being rushed, and general morale. If, for instance, office workers leave on time, and blue collar workers leave later, it may mean a rush project is forcing the latter to stay late. The type of attire may give a clue to the type of project. Many people leaving early may mean little work or low morale.

A panorama shot can provide relative location of shops in the facility as well as distances. Medium shots can cover particular work areas, while close ups can identify people and their attire.

Equipment

Photograph construction equipment, kilns, generators, pump houses, furnaces, machine tools, etc.

Note features, size, fabrication, and capacity. Photograph the equipment to show use and relationship to overall activity. Try to identify manufacturer and whether or not it is new or used. Note any equipment being repaired or standing idle. Photograph any signs of retooling for a new product.

Use medium shots to place equipment and close-ups to show detail.

Support Required

Photos should show power requirements, transportation, raw materials, and other companies in the area that provide services or support.

Emphasize the type of support required and the volume. Photograph the type of transportation (rail, road, air) and its overall capacity. Photographing the number of railcars and trucks can give an idea of capacity and backlog. Photograph piles of coal or raw materials and include measurements. Identify the source of the power supply. Photograph shipping activity.

Distant shots should tie-in support services, while medium and close-up photos should detail the type.

Products

Photos should emphasize the type of product, size, shape, and the number that may be on loading docks, etc. Also photograph raw materials (photos should indicate dimensions of the stockpile) and try to obtain a close-up to determine its grade.

Medium and close-up shots can identify the product, storage, and handling.

Storage

Photograph the type of material stored, methods, capacities, and other unusual features.

Distant shots can show location, accessibility, and relationship to the plant, while close-ups show methods and materials.

Construction Sites

Construction Techniques

Photograph foundations, load-bearing walls, columns, frames, girders, trusses, anchors, abutments, etc.

Your photographs should identify the manner in which materials are used to achieve strength, rigidity, elasticity, loading, and damage.

Use medium shots to show fabrication, and close-ups to show bonding, joints, and kinds of structural members.

Construction Site

Photos should show layout, equipment installation, power distribution, and roads.

Photos should emphasize the future use of the various parts of the site. Heavy equipment may be installed before construction is complete, electric lines show where power consumption is, different construction methods may indicate where heavy equipment will be installed, extra ventilation may indicate the future computer center or a clean room, and roads may indicate the loading dock. Photographing the site with workers will allow interpreters to judge distances.

Use distant shots to show general layout. Medium or close-up shots can identify features.

Office Buildings

Photos should emphasize general character of the building. Photos of the parking lot can identify the number and type of workers and the type of vendors that deal with the people in the building. Unusual features should be noted (e.g. antenna or satellite dishes on the roof).

Photographing the people can identify the type of jobs, and relationships to each other (see the section on factories). Photographing the bumper stickers and decals on cars can identify schools and professions (engineering schools, professional societies, etc.).

Photos should be either medium shots to show the general characteristics of the building or parking lot, or close-ups of people or unusual features. Because office buildings are hard to identify, include as much material with the photos as possible.

6

Documenting
The Photographs

Good photographs are worthless without notes. If you don't supply data, you just have snapshots. Provide good information, and you have an important intelligence source.

Although it may be tempting to postpone the note taking until later, the best notes are taken as the photographs are made. You forget too many important facts if you wait. The only exception would be if you are in a hostile area where notes would compromise you. In that case, a simple code might help.

Some data will be valid for the whole mission. Other information will have to be noted with each shot. After each photograph write down the exposure, and then include any important information. The following information should be included in your notes:

- Lens — The focal length of the lens is essential to taking measurements from the photograph. If you are using a zoom lens, estimate the focal length.

- Exposure — If the length of the exposure and the distance are available, an interpreter can estimate the speed of an object in the photo by measuring the blur.

If you are using this method to judge speed, take long exposures and shoot several photographs.

- Camera Bearing — This is the direction the camera is pointing.

- Time and Date — Give the day and time the photographs are taken. Local time should be used if different time zones are involved.

- Miscellaneous Photographic Data — Note filters, auxiliary equipment, and the type of film used.

- Distance — Note distance from the camera to the object. Include the dimensions of any objects in the photograph (if known).

- Geographic Information — Give enough information to accurately locate the site. You will look pretty stupid if you deliver an excellent piece of intelligence, but forget where it was taken. Location information can include country, town, longitude, latitude, street or any other information that can pinpoint the location. Add bearings and distances to major landmarks. Include a copy of the map if you use one.

- Name of the Activity — Give the complete and exact name for the site.

- Remarks — Describe the activity, the characteristic features, and actions taking place. Evaluate its importance. Report changes or unusual activity. Identify all possible structures. Include all distances and relationships to other facilities. Note directions to other related activities. Compare it to additional photos if necessary. It's a good idea to put as much information as possible on a copy of the photograph when sending in the report.

Figure 6-1

Always annotate photos. The viewer might miss the submarine in the lower left-hand corner of this shot.

7

Collecting
Additional Information

As the last chapter revealed, the photograph is only part of photographic intelligence. The are many methods for collecting additional information that can support the photo or can even be used without a camera.

Even a country that has stringent controls on movement and cameras can reveal information, if the gatherer is persistent. Journals often contain stories of new processes or facilities that can supplement a photographic intelligence mission. Although the photos, figures, and information may be misleading, by combining them with your work, they may prove important.

Professional photographers usually take the photos for postcards and scenic folders. Don't underestimate the value of these photos. They are usually well focused and properly exposed and a selection of these shots can provide valuable information, especially about beaches and important cities. They can save the time and risk of a mission.

Noting the distances in a photograph is easier if you know the dimensions of some well-known objects. Some of these are:

- Sizes of athletic fields.
- Railroad equipment.
- Well-known landmarks.
- Well-known buildings.

You should also know these personal measurements:

- Height.
- Pace.
- Shoe length.
- Length of arm from eye to fingertip.
- Length of thumb tip and various fingers.
- Height of various body parts, such as knees, groin, navel, armpit, and chin.

You can judge distance with a compass and a ruler. A range finder can also help although they may be limited in the distances they cover.

If these items aren't available, you can substitute a conventional watch (with a face), and some item with a known length. Remember the dimensions of cigarettes, paper clips, and matches. If you carry a Swiss army knife, you probably have a ruler.

Determining An Unknown Measurement

You can determine an unknown measurement by using simple proportions and three other known values. This is useful in determining heights and widths of unknown objects. The only equipment needed is a ruler. You must know any three of these values to determine the fourth:

a = length sighted on the scale (inches)

b = distance from the eye to the ruler (in inches)

B = distance from observer to object (in feet)

A = measurement of object in feet

Procedure:

1. Sight object across the ruler and determine the length (see Figure 7-1).

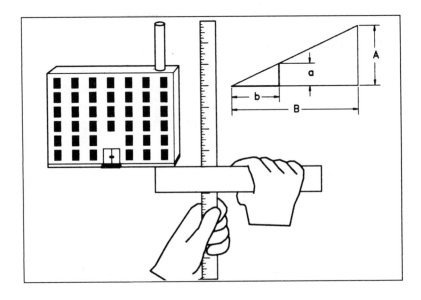

Figure 7-1

Determining an unknown measurement using three known values.

2. Determine distance from observer to object.

3. Substitute values in this formula:

$$\frac{a}{b} = \frac{A \times 12}{B \times 12}$$

4. If a = 1.5 inches, b = 21 inches, and B = 980 ft, then

$$\frac{1.5}{21} = \frac{A \times 12}{980 \times 12}$$

Therefore, A = 70 feet

If A is known, then the distance to the object (B) can be also determined.

Determining Height

The unknown height of an object can be determined by using the principle of proportional triangles. The shadow cast by the object can be measured and the height and shadow of a measuring unit can be determined. Again, the only item required is a measuring unit. The variables are:

a   =   height of measuring unit

b   =   length of measuring unit's shadow

B   =   length of object's shadow

A   =   height of object

Procedure:

1. Pace off or measure the length of the object's shadow.

2. Position the measuring unit and measure its shadow.

3. If security considerations prevent you from using a measuring unit, note the time of day and measure it elsewhere the next day. The shadow of the observer is also a good choice.

    Substitute the known values in this equation:

$$\frac{a}{b} = \frac{A \times 12}{B \times 12}$$

If a = 6 inches, b = 9 inches, and B = 126 feet, then,

$$\frac{6}{9} = \frac{A \times 12}{126 \times 12};$$ or if you are using the observer as the measuring unit, then the height of the observer is 6 feet and the shadow is 9 feet. Then 6/9 = A/126 or A = 84 feet.

Determining Distances Without a Ruler

Napoleon promoted a soldier in his army for this idea. Use a baseball cap or other hat with a brim. Sight at the base of the object and move the brim of the hat down on the forehead until it appears to touch the object's base. Turn around and locate where the tip of the brim appears to touch. Pace that distance. It should be approximately the same as the distance to the object. This will only work on relatively flat ground.

Determining Measurements With a Window

This is a modification of the first method. Instead of using a ruler, you mark the scale on a windshield of a car or the window of a train. As you pass objects you can determine measurements by using the formula mentioned earlier. You must be careful to keep your head in the same position and you must correct for any angle in the windshield.

Measuring Using the Barleon Method

The distance from an observer to a reference object can be determined if a dimension of the object is known. The only equipment needed is a pencil or other straight object. The variables are:

a   =   distance between the pupils of the eyes

b   =   distance from the eye to a hand-held pencil

r   =   b/a is used as a constant. An approximation of 10 is often used

A   =   height or width of the object

c-c'   =   the numerical relation between the height or width of the object and the distance it appears to move during sighting when the observer changes his sighting eye

B   =   distance from the observer to the object

Procedure:

1. Using the right eye, sight the pencil on the object.

2. Slide the thumbnail along the pencil until the distance between it and the pencil end intercepts the known height or width of the object. The distance on the pencil is your measuring unit (Figure 7-2).

3. Without moving the pencil, close your right eye and sight with the left eye. The pencil will appear to move from position c to position c'.

4. Turn the pencil and measure c to c' using the measurement you established on the pencil.

5. Substitute the known values in these formulae:

   $r = b/a$ (this can be measured or you can use the constant 10); $B = A \times r \times (c\text{-}c')$. If $A = 84$ feet, $c\text{-}c' = 2.5$, and $r = 10$, then $B = 2100$ feet.

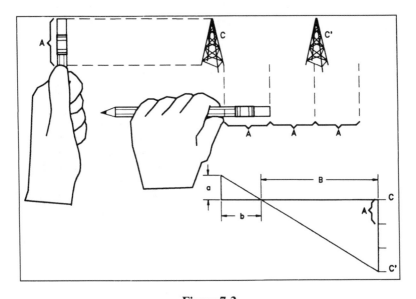

Figure 7-2

Determining the distance between observer and object using the Barleon Method.

Other Measuring Devices

Anyone who has taken trigonometry knows other methods for determining distance and angle. Rather than rehash each one of them, I will just say that a protractor and a chart of sines, cosines, and tangents will help you immeasurably. If you don't have a protractor, a conventional watch can substitute. Just remember each minute is equal to 6 degrees.

An example of using a protractor (or watch) and a tangent would be the following. You are traveling alongside a target. Using your protractor or watch, take a bearing of the object (the direction you are traveling is 0 degrees). Measure the distance you travel until you are abeam of the target (directly to your left or right). The tangent of the angle you measured times the distance traveled is equal to the distance from the vehicle to the target (see Figure 7-3).

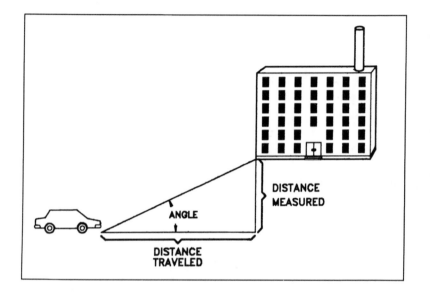

Figure 7-3

Determining the distance between observer and
object using a known angle and a known distance.

Example: You sight a factory just off to your left and the bearing is 50 degrees from the direction you are traveling. You then travel 2,000 feet until the site is just directly to your left. The tangent of 50 degrees is 1.1918, so you multiply the 1.1918 times 2,000 ft. The result shows that the factory is 2,383 feet away from your second sighting. Of course, this method is only as good as your method for measuring distance, so something more accurate than an odometer is recommended. If your speedometer is accurate, you can determine distance traveled with a stopwatch.

Distance to the Horizon

This method is useful in flatlands or on the sea shore. A rule of thumb is that the distance to the horizon in miles is the square root of the height of the eye in feet times 1.31. The following table gives height and distance to the horizon in feet and miles.

HEIGHT	MILES	FEET
6	3.22	17,023
10	4.14	21,887
15	5.06	26,751
50	9.32	49,247
100	13.12	69,311

Determining Slope

Determining slope can be important in reporting on amphibious or airborne assault targets. This method requires two observers or one observer and a movable object of known height. Three variables are required:

a = pacer's height

b = height of observer's eye

c = horizontal distance (measured by pacer)

Procedure:

1. The observer sits down facing the downward part of the slope (see Figure 7-4).

2. The pacer, counting the steps, moves down the slope.

3. When the observer's line of sight to the horizon passes over the pacer's head, the observer signals.

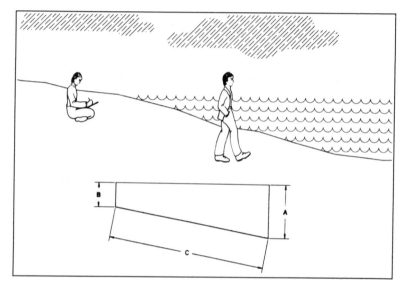

Figure 7-4

Using two people to determine the slope of the hill or grade.

4. The pacer returns and rechecks the distance.

5. The distance paced by the one person should not differ markedly unless the slope is 1:4 or steeper.

6. The gradient = (a-b)/c

7. If a = 6 feet, b = 2 feet, and c = 80 feet; then the gradient is (6-2)/80, or 1:20.

8

Copying Documents

This is a typical scene from the movies. A spy enters a room, cracks the safe, lays the papers out on the desk, turns on the desk lamp, and quickly flips through the pages as he snaps away with a miniature camera. Can this really happen? Sure, if the desk lamp is a spotlight or the secret documents were written with crayons.

These scenarios gloss over the problems. There is too little light, focusing is too critical, and film resolution isn't good enough for the small size of the spy camera film.

Since this type of photography isn't realistic, we will ignore it. However, if you are in such a situation, I suggest you go down the hall and use the copier. The other option is to buy a pocket copier from an electronics or office supply store.

However, if you can keep the papers for a little while and you need to carry copies through a border, a film canister might be less conspicuous. Copying documents is also a good idea if you want to condense some information to eliminate paper around the office. But the most important aspect of copying a document is that you can make it clearer than the original. There are even some techniques for detecting forgeries or altered documents.

Copying documents with your 35mm camera is easy. You buy a macro lens, a close-up lens, or extension bellows. Then you purchase a copy stand (available from most camera stores) and photo lamps. A more detailed review of the equipment and mechanics of close-up photography can be found in a good book on cameras.

The following are common types of documents that you may need to copy. Much of this information is available in the Kodak book on copying. The address for it and other Kodak books is in Appendix II.

- *Pencil Sketches.* Although these are line drawings, the shadings can be lost or made darker under some circumstances. A moderately high contrast film like Kodak Contrast Process Ortho Film 4154 (Ektar thick Base) is best. It should be exposed and developed for medium contrast to preserve the density of the lines.

- *Printed Matter.* Kodak *Kodalith* film is best for reproducing lines. If the lines are fine, develop with *Kodalith* Fine-line developer. If the original is on thin paper and is only printed on one side, put a sheet of white paper behind it when exposing it. If it is printed on both sides, use a sheet of black paper to keep the other side from showing. If you want to make micro-film, the most readily available film is Technical Pan Film 2415.

- *Drawings.* Drawings should be copied in the same way as printed material. If the lines are faint, use a high contrast film like Kodak high contrast copy 5069.

- *Typewritten Originals.* Should be treated similar to drawings.

- *Blueprints.* These should be copied with a panchromatic film with a red filter (Kodak Wratten filter No. 25 or 29). The blue background will record as black while the lines remain white.

- *Handwritten Manuscripts.* Copy the same way as you would a sketch. If the manuscript is written with a pencil, print on a high contrast paper.

- *Checks and Money Orders.* Use Kodak Contrast process pan film 4155 (Ektar Thick Base).

- *Yellowed Documents.* Yellowed documents with black or grey ink require high contrast orthochromatic or panchromatic film and a deep-yellow filter like a Kodak Wratten Filter No. 15. The copy will appear clearer than the original.

- *Faded Documents.* Faded documents and ink require Kodak Commercial Film 6127 or Contrast Process Pan Film with a blue (No. 47) filter.

- *Suspected Forgeries.* Forgeries should be copied with infrared film to reveal the original condition. More will be covered in the infrared photography chapter.

- *Detecting Vanished Writing.* Ultraviolet light can detect some erasures and faded writing. A dark room, an ultraviolet source, a Kodak Wratten Filter No. 2A, and your camera are all that is needed. The exposures should be bracketed between 10 seconds and 1 minute with a setting of f/16. The best film is Kodak Contrast Process Ortho Film. Some ultra violet sources allow too much visible light. If that is true of yours, put the light in a light-tight box with a window made of a 10mm Corning Glass Filter No. 5860.

9

Aerial Photography

Mention the word aerial photography, and images of spy satellites and supersonic reconnaissance aircraft come to mind. Today the superpowers have a surprising array of tools for overhead photography, like the U.S.'s KH-12, a spy satellite so large it can only be launched by the space shuttle. Can the "small time" operator hope to equal its resolution?

Because the size and the technology of spy satellites are known, we can make a guess at the theoretical resolution. By using the equation given in the resolution chapter, an orbit of 275 kilometers, a focal length of 57.6 meters (limited by the size of the shuttle's cargo bay), and a pixel resolution of .0015 centimeters, a theoretical resolution of 7.16cm was arrived at. That is a resolution of less than three inches. Of course, that figure may be a little better because the pixel size of advanced spy satellites may be smaller than we think. However, it probably isn't any better than 1 to 2 inches. That makes it possible for intelligence services to identify equipment and even see if a soldier is reading a newspaper! But your properly planned aerial shots with a 35mm can easily duplicate that (even if they aren't in the U.S.S.R.).

Aerial photographs offer several advantages. They are accurate in determining distance, positions, and heights. They can cover large areas and have map-like qualities. They can often notice things that can't be seen from the ground. And finally, aircraft can fly over or near restricted areas.

For example, according to the horizon measuring formula given in Chapter 7, a plane flying a mile above the surface can see objects on the horizon that are over seventy miles away. If you use a 500mm lens and a film that gives you a resolution of 300 lines per millimeter, your theoretical resolution of that object 70 miles away is 30 inches! Of course, this is the theoretical resolution and doesn't consider weather conditions, haze, camera quality, or aircraft movement, but it would give you the opportunity to identify large objects like buildings or some military equipment in an area that is restricted to you. Of course, this resolution is just a tenth as good as what the government can achieve, but it's available for hundreds of dollars instead of hundreds of millions of dollars. We will say more about this in the chapter on resolution.

Although special equipment is usually used in aerial photography, good results can be expected from your 35mm SLR. The most important factor, as with other missions, is to plan in advance.

The most important decision to be made concerns the scale of the photo. This is the ratio of the ground photographed to the image on the negative. Obviously the higher you fly, the larger the scale, but you must also allow for the type of lens you are shooting with. The scale can be calculated by dividing the focal length of the lens by the altitude of the aircraft. Therefore, a 100mm lens used at 1,500 meters is 100/1,500,000 or 1:15,000. That means 15,000 inches (or 1250 feet) equals one inch in the negative.

Once you have the scale, you can calculate the distance covered in the negative. That will allow you to plan overlapping photos. If your calculations show each negative covers 2,000 feet, then you should plan to take a shot every time the plane traverses about 1,500 feet (unless you want stereo coverage, in which case you must have a 60% overlap and shoot every 800 feet). If the ground speed of the craft is 120 mph, then you are covering 10,560 feet a minute. That means you should shoot 7 times a minute or about every eight seconds.

Problems

The photographer must also be prepared for some problems with aerial photography. Following are some more common ones and recommendations for eliminating them.

Haze

Haze can diminish resolution and cut down on the contrast in the picture. The photographer can counter this in black and white film by using a yellow filter to limit the amount of blue light reaching the film. In color film the correction must be more subtle, and consequently, isn't as effective. The Kodak Haze Cutting Filters HF-3 and HF-4 are effective for this purpose. You can also use infrared film, although it will not act the same as regular film.

Motion

Any aircraft will have some motion. There will be the forward motion of a fixed wing aircraft and the machinery motion that occurs in both fixed wing aircraft and helicopters. There are several ways to dampen these effects. Machinery motion can be limited by keeping the camera and the upper part of the torso away from contact with the aircraft. Another, more expensive solution, is a gyrostabilizer. This allows you to hand hold with longer lenses and for longer exposures. Another option that appears to be innocent is a hot air balloon. Although they can't be directed, they eliminate machinery noise and are slower than conventional aircraft. That makes them excellent platforms for high resolution photos.

The forward motion of an aircraft can be limited by the pilot by flying into the wind as you go over the target. The motion can also be limited by flying at higher altitudes, although this will reduce resolution.

You can also eliminate motion with faster film, shorter exposures, or more sunlight on the target.

Clouds

Clouds can ruin a mission if the target is covered. Even if not fully covered, the patches of sunlight and dark may require more latitude than the film allows. The best way to avoid this is to contact the airport for a weather report and design your mission to be under the cloud cover if possible.

Water

Water is often the target of a photograph, but from the air, streams and rivers can be hidden by vegetation. Since water absorbs infrared light, infrared film is excellent for delineating water boundaries.

Seasons

The success of the mission can often depend on the season. Aerial photographers often wait until the leaves have fallen from the trees before taking shots.

Equipment Recommendations

Film

Although you can use most films in aerial photography, they aren't designed for the mission. Kodak makes aerial films that have greater latitude and higher contrast than most films. Unfortunately, these are hard to find, expensive, may require large orders, and may not come in 35mm size. Information on those currently available from Kodak can be obtained from Kodak publication M-29, *Kodak Data for Aerial Photography.* Another tool for the serious student is the Kodak Aerial Exposure Computer.

For those who can't acquire the special aerial film or who don't want to make their plans known, Kodak Plus-X film is very similar to Kodak Plus-X Aerographic.

Filters

Filters are commonly used in aerial photography in order to eliminate haze, or other parts of the color spectrum. Earlier we talked about how to eliminate haze with yellow filters. One that may also be used for black and white film is the red Kodak filter No. 25. This will eliminate more of the blue color. This filter is also used when taking photos with infrared film. If you want to eliminate more of the visible spectrum, the dark red No. 70 is available or the No. 89B, which blocks out all visible radiation.

Aircraft

Any aircraft can provide acceptable photos. However, certain types are easier to work with. Obviously, one that can fly without a door can be helpful in photography. Usually these are high wing aircraft, so they are good because the wing isn't an obstruction like in a low wing plane. High wing aircraft are also better because they have lower minimum flying speeds than others. You should check several aircraft because some have modifications to allow photography.

Helicopters offer a slower speed for taking critical photos. However, the cost of renting one (over $1,000 per hour) is beyond most budgets. A strong head wind and a plane with a low minimum flying speed can provide as good a platform as a hovering helicopter.

Obviously, aerial photography can be much more complicated than shown here. However, the equipment required is expensive and would attract attention. Since the purpose of this book is to provide intelligence photographs with inexpensive equipment while maintaining a low profile, I recommend that those interested in more advanced information purchase the books available from Kodak.

10

Infrared Photography

Infrared photography is a useful tool for intelligence purposes, but it is also very misunderstood. Before we go into the uses of infrafred film, let's review some things it can and cannot do:

- Infrared film can take pictures in what appears to be total darkness.

- Infrared film cannot take pictures in total darkness without an infrared light source.

- Infrared film doesn't require special photographic equipment.

- Infrared film can't photograph hot objects, unless their temperature is over 482 degrees Fahrenheit (if they are over 932 degrees Fahrenheit, you can see a visible glow). Even then, it may take minutes for the object to register on film.

- Infrared film is best able to record reflected infrared light. Most natural infrared sources produce so little light as to make photography difficult.

Having clarified what this type of film can do, let's go into the theory and practice of infrared photography.

Theory

As you know from physics, the light we see is just the visible spectrum, ranging from 400 to 700 nanometers wavelength. Electromagnetic energy that falls below 400nm is ultraviolet, and that which lies just above 700nm is infrared. Although some equipment and materials can detect more of the infrared spectrum, infrared film only detects the part of the infrared spectrum nearest visible light (700 to 900nm). Consequently, much of the infrared spectrum, including that emitted by the human body, is invisible to this film. That is not to say that a more sensitive film couldn't be made, but handling regular infrared film is enough trouble. For instance, it must be loaded in the dark and kept in the refrigerator.

As I said earlier, infrared film is best able to record reflected light. That means it's best at noting the differences between reflected visible light and infrared light since it also records the rest of the visible spectrum. That allows you to compare the different reflectance just as you can compare the reflectance between a shiny object and one that is a flat black. This can be useful in comparing the difference between camouflage and natural foliage.

Applications

Infrared film can be used in many applications. I will discuss some of those that are more critical to intelligence missions. A more detailed coverage of this field can be found in Kodak's book *Applied Infrared Photography* (M-28).

Effects on Foliage

Chlorophyll reflects infrared light and appears light in B & W photos. Plants that are ill or under stress have less chlorophyll and reflect less infrared. Since this is used to determine diseased plants, infrared film can be used to identify chemical factories. Many chemicals will affect the health of surrounding plants. Consequently, exhausts and pipes dumping waste can be identified by analyzing infrared photos. In color infrared film, cyan is the color of such poisoned plants, while magenta-red is the color of healthy plants. Sewage can also be tracked in a large river because clean water is black while chemical sewage may be red or milky.

Underground facilities can also be identified and sized by studying the changes in plants caused by waste, heat, and drainage. This can be especially helpful in aerial photography.

Haze

Haze obscures details, especially in distant objects. Since infrared light is less likely to be scattered by haze, distant scenes will be much sharper with infrared film.

Obscured Writing

Documents may be illegible because of age, deterioration, erasing, invisible inks, or applying something on top of the original. Although many of these appear hard to read, they are often different in terms of their ability to reflect infrared. Photos of these documents can discover writing that has been crossed out, written in invisible ink, added to an original, charred by fire, or made difficult to read because of age. Equipment can be photographed in order to read data that has worn off or has been obliterated. In fact, this is such a valuable use of infrared film, that any item that may have been altered can be examined with a set of infrared photos.

Night Photography

Night photography allows you to take shots without arousing suspicion or to observe an activity that can't be photographed in the light. A Kodak Wratten Filter No. 87 or 87C can be placed over a flash attachment (with a light-tight housing) to make it an infrared source. Since the internal exposure meter isn't going to operate properly, it would be wise to experiment with it first and bracket the exposure. Like regular flash units, their distance is limited and the maximum that can be covered is probably 60 feet with a powerful flash unit.

Camouflage

Although camouflage appears to be the same color as the surrounding area, the lack of chlorophyll makes it appear different in infrared photos.

Burned Documents

Documents that have been charred beyond recognition or the intact ash of burned documents can often be read by photographing them with infrared film. Since an intact ash is usually warped, the photographer must use a small aperture in order to have the greatest depth of field.

Protecting Information

If there is a chance photographed documents may be captured and read, you may want to use infrared film. If they are confiscated by the enemy, the person opening the film container in the light (and most agents will inspect the plastic film container as soon as they find it) will destroy the image because the 35mm film cartridge doesn't protect the film from infrared light (that's why you must load the camera in the dark). You can protect yourself more by using an unmarked film cartridge and just exposing the first few frames of film (that helps insure that some infrared light reaches all the exposed film).

11

Choosing
The Right Film

There isn't a "correct" film, since the choice depends on the mission. While picture quality is the most important thing, this is colored by other circumstances like whether or not you have to shoot a moving vehicle, the amount of light when the photo is taken, and whether you can use a tripod.

The best way to choose the ideal film is to have enough information on the film types that you will most likely have available. What follows is a synopsis of the major Kodak films (and one from Fuji) and the information most likely to be of use to someone in the intelligence field. I have made a judgement as to their use for intelligence purposes. This doesn't mean ones that are ranked poor shouldn't be used. It only means that the photos can't be enlarged for detailed study. They are still excellent choices for situations where speed is needed. However, if the speed isn't required, it may be wise to choose another film.

Color Print Film

Kodacolor 100 Film

This is the sharpest and most widely available film you can find. It may found at supermarkets and drug stores in most of the world. It is designed for the amateur, so it has a great deal of exposure latitude. It is developed with the conventional C-41 process. This film can resolve up to 100 lines per mm and has high definition for intelligence purposes.

Kodacolor 200 Film

This is another popular print film found in many stores. It has a great deal of exposure latitude, but not as much as the VR 100. The film is developed with the C-41 process. This film can resolve up to 100 lines per mm and has high definition for intelligence purposes.

Kodacolor 400 Film

This is a very fast film which makes it good for photographing in low light situations. It is balanced to give good color inside or outdoors. Uses the C-41 process. This film can resolve up to 80 lines and has poor definition for intelligence purposes.

Kodacolor 1000 Film

This is the fastest of the Kodacolor line and is useful indoors. It is color balanced to give good color both outdoors and indoors. Uses the C-41 process. This film can resolve up to 80 lines per mm and has poor definition for intelligence purposes.

Ektar 25

This is the latest addition to Kodak's line of print films. It has the highest resolution and definition ever found in a color print film. The Ektar line is only found at camera stores at the moment, but it will become readily available as it replaces the Kodacolor line. It uses the C-41 process. The film can resolve up to 200 lines per mm and has a very high definition for intelligence purposes.

Ektar 125

This is the medium film in the Ektar line. It uses the same technology, so it has the same high definition characteristics of the rest of the line, but has more latitude than the Ektar 25. It uses the C-41 process. The film can resolve up to 160 lines and has very high definition for intelligence purposes.

Ektar 1000

This is the fast film in the Ektar line and provides the best definition of the fast color print films. It provides an excellent balance between definition and speed. It uses the C-41 process. This film can resolve up to 80 lines per mm and has a poor definition for intelligence purposes.

Kodacolor 1600

This film hadn't been released as this book was being written. According to the company, it will replace the Kodacolor 1000. Since it uses some Ektar technology, it is expected to have better definition than the Kodacolor 400. It will use the C-41 process.

Color Transparencies

Kodachrome 25

This has been considered the standard for definition, color saturation, and archival quality. This is a good choice when color is needed in the photograph.The development process is complicated and requires expensive equipment. Therefore, the film will have to be developed through a processing lab. The film has a resolving power of 100 lines per mm and has a very high definition for intelligence purposes.

Kodachrome 64

This is a medium speed film of the Kodachrome family. Although the definition is a bit less than Kodachrome 25, it still has the same color saturation, and durability. It requires a special developing process that is only available from processing labs. The film has a resolving power of 100mm and has a very high definition for intelligence purposes.

Fujichrome 50

This is challenging Kodachrome 25 as the best color transparency film. It has good color saturation and higher resolution in high contrast situations (lower in low contrast situations). It is developed with the E-6 process. This film has a resolution of 120 lines per mm and has a very high definition for intelligence purposes.

Ektachrome 64

A good general film. It is developed with the E-6 process. This film has a resolution of 125 lines per mm and has medium definition for intelligence purposes.

Ektachrome 400

A high speed film for dim situations or fast action. It is designed for outdoors situations, but can be used under carbon arc lamps without a loss in color. It is developed with the E-6 process. This film has a resolution of 80 lines per mm and has poor definition for intelligence purposes.

Ektachrome P800/1600

This is a high speed film designed for pushing to higher speeds. It can even provide acceptable results at EI 3200. It is developed with the E-6 process, although processing times must be changed if the film has been pushed. This film has a resolution of 80, 63, and 63 lines per mm at the respective speeds of 800, 1600, and 3200. It has poor definition for intelligence purposes.

Ektachrome Infrared Slide Film

This produces false color transparencies. Ordinary film-speed ratings don't apply because exposure meters don't measure infrared accurately. This film must be loaded in the dark and processed soon after exposure. This film is developed with the E-4 process. The resolution of the film is 80 lines per mm and it has poor definition for intelligence purposes.

Black and White Film

Plus-X pan Film

This is a general purpose panchromatic film that offers a good combination of speed and definition. It has an ISO of 125 and can be processed with normal B & W methods (Microdol-X recommended). The film has a resolution of 125 lines per mm and a high definition for intelligence purposes.

Panatomic-X Film

This is an extremely fine grained film. It has an ISO of 32 and can be processed with normal B & W methods (Microdol-X recommended). This film has a resolution of 200 lines per mm and a very high definition for intelligence purposes.

Kodak Tri-X Film

A high speed B & W film. It has an ISO of 400 and can be processed with normal B & W methods (Microdol-X recommended). This film has a resolution of 100 lines per mm and a poor definition for intelligence purposes.

Kodak High Speed Infrared Film 2481

This is a high contrast film that is useful in most cases where an infrared film is needed. It is not possible to give an exact ISO because exposure meters don't accurately measure infrared light. However, a figure of 80 can be used in daylight with no filter. This film is difficult to handle. It must be loaded in the complete dark and stored at 55 degrees Fahrenheit. Keep away from heat. Develop immediately after exposing. It should be developed with D-76. This film has a resolving power of 80 lines per mm and has poor definition for intelligence purposes.

T-MAX 100

This is the latest B & W technology from Kodak. By using a T-Grain emulsion technology, they have made a faster film that has better definition. It can be developed with regular B & W processes although Kodak T-MAX developer will give the best results. This film has a resolution of 200 lines per mm and a very high definition for intelligence purposes.

T-MAX 400

This is the general high speed film of the T-MAX series. It can be developed with regular B & W processes although Kodak T-MAX developer is recommended. This film has a resolution of 125 lines per mm and a high definition for intelligence purposes.

T-MAX 3200

A very high speed film that can provide film speeds of up to EI 25,000, although it is recommended for use at 3200 or 6400. It can be developed with regular B & W processes although Kodak T-MAX is recommended. Resolution depends on the speed used. It has a poor definition for intelligence purposes.

Technical Pan Film 2415

This film has the best definition of all films readily available. It can be used to make microfilm of documents or drawings. Its film speed depends on the application, although 25 is acceptable for pictorial purposes and 325 for printed matter. It uses regular B & W development processes, although the type of developer depends on the use. For pictures, Technidol liquid developer is recommended and can provide a resolution of 320 lines per mm. It has extremely high definition for intelligence purposes.

12

Developing Film

Many photographic intelligence photos can't be developed at a lab because of their subject or the speed with which they are needed. That means the photographer must occasionally be able to process the film himself. Yet that scares most people. Visions of darkrooms, chemicals, and expense make developing a black art. However, developing is easy, the equipment can fit into a brief case, and the chemicals and equipment can be bought for the price of developing 6 rolls of film with a processing laboratory.

Rather than getting into the details of developing film, which is covered by many other books, I will just cover methods for developing film quickly, secretly, and with the minimum of equipment.

I will not go into prints, because they require a second step (going from negative to print), and photo interpreters as a rule prefer to study the original (transparency or negative) because it provides more resolution. If your work requires a print and you need to process it quickly and without a darkroom, I recommend the Daylab 300 by Daylab Ltd.

Processing film anywhere in the world is easy if you have a developing tank, a thermometer, a changing bag, a watch with a second hand, the chemicals, and some way to measure the chemicals. If you reuse the chemicals, you may want some storage containers. A picnic cooler would also be nice, but not necessary, if you want better temperature control.

Acquiring the chemicals is easy. Kodak produces "hobby pacs" for the E-6 process, C-41 process, and B & W developing. They contain premeasured chemicals for developing about 6 rolls and instructions for the rankest beginner. These packs are available at most camera stores.

Although all C-41, E-6, and B & W films can be processed anywhere, the best for undercover purposes is slide film (E-6). Slides can be developed and available for viewing in about half an hour. Black and white negatives are easier, but many people have a hard time evaluating negatives.

I will not go into the details of developing, but I will review the basics. Slide film that uses the E-6 process undergoes 4 steps: developer, color bleach, bleach fix, and stabilizer. The film is put into the changing bag with the developing tank. The film is taken out of the cartridge with a bottle opener. It is then rolled on the reel while in the changing bag (practice this loading first before doing it blind). The top is put on the tank and the bag can be opened. Each developing step consists of adding the chemical, occasionally agitating it, removing the chemical after a set time, and washing the film. After the stabilizer, a wetting agent can be added to keep the film from streaking. Now the film is removed from the tank and is hung up to dry. Although a little cloudy, it can be viewed then.

Excellent results can be achieved anywhere. The temperature at which you process the film can range from 75 to 110 degrees Fahrenheit. The only important point is to keep the temperature constant once you start. This means you can develop film in hotel rooms or even out in the field (in fact, the photos I took for this book were developed on a picnic table in the Arizona desert). All you need is a fire to warm the water, and a cooler to maintain the temperature of the water and chemicals. If you process black and white negatives, you can use room temperature water and avoid the need for a cooler.

Although film processing can be more complicated, these are the basics for processing film quickly, anywhere and with better quality than is usually available. It is a critical part of good photographic intelligence. It will give you better results, provide a higher level of security, and will prove cheaper than if you had a processing lab handle it.

13

Measurement
and Resolution

For the photos in this book, the photographer was asked to provide the distance from the camera to the target and the focal length of the lens. The reason was to give the analyst the opportunity to measure the dimensions of the target or the surrounding area. The key to this is the equation: Scale = distance/ focal length.

Example: A target 500 meters away was photographed with a 200mm lens. The equation becomes: Scale = 500,000/ 200mm, which gives a scale of 1:2500. That means one millimeter on the film equals 2500mm at the target or 2.5 meters. If the photo is of an airfield and an aircraft image is 5mm long on the film, then the aircraft is 12.5 meters long. This is an important tool in analyzing targets. Even if the distance is unknown, as long as the lens focal length was in the information, an analyst can judge distance by using a derivative of the formula and determining scale from a known object (like a person) at the distance desired.

The same formula can also be used to calculate resolution. But before we go into determining resolution, let's look at it and what it can do for you.

Resolution is the smallest size an item can be and still be seen in a photo. In the film chapter, we indicated film resolution by showing how many lines per millimeter the film could resolve in a high contrast situation. In that case the number represented the smallest a line could be and still be recognized as a line. In photographic intelligence this represents the finest resolution you can obtain under ideal conditions (later we will talk about some methods for stretching that value).

Many factors must be taken into account before you can use that resolution figure as the basis for determining the quality of your photos. The first factor is the contrast of the photo. The resolution number in the previous chapter represents a high contrast situation. In other words, it can define a line if it is pure black, the surrounding area is pure white and the scene is well lit. That is only significant if you are photographing antennas against a sunny sky. The resolution in low contrast situations is usually two thirds to one half the number given in the previous chapter (about 66 to 50 lines per mm if the original number was 100 lines per mm). That number may even drop more if there is a very mild contrast (identifying the maintenance panel of an aircraft). Other factors inherent in the film are sharpness and grain. These, along with resolution, will decide if the picture and the objects in it are sharp or whether they appear as indefinable blobs. In this book, I've called it definition for intelligence purposes. That doesn't mean the films I ranked as poor can't be used. It just means they have limited value in detailed analysis.

While the film sets the highest value your photo can reach, your camera, lens, filters, tripod, accessories, and atmospheric conditions cut that value down. This is where the expensive equipment shows its value. Well chosen equipment can keep the resolution as high as possible.

The biggest and most expensive obstacle to fine resolution is the lens. As a rule of thumb, your lens must have three times the resolution of the film in order to achieve maximum resolution. Therefore, your lens must have a resolution of 300 lines per mm in order to guarantee 100 lines per mm. If you check out lens tests in photo magazines, you realize that requires good quality optics.

There are some ways to improve lens resolution without spending too much money. The most important point to remember is that glass limits the amount of light reaching the film and therefore limits resolution. Therefore, sharper lenses have fewer elements than others have. That immediately cuts out zoom lenses because they need more elements. The sharpest lens will have fixed focal length. Of the fixed focal length lenses, the best will be the long barrel ones, instead of shorter ones with mirrors or additional glass.

Having removed most of the glass from the lens, it is silly to add more in the way of filters, unless they are critical to the job. Skylight filters, often used for protection, should be removed for high resolution shots.

The aperture also has an impact on sharpness. Left too wide open or too small, the aperture will limit the resolution of your shots. The best f-stop is two full stops from the widest opening.

You now have the sharpest lens, the finest resolution film, and the optimum aperture. All that is worthless if you hand hold the camera. Even the steadiest hand will scrub a few mm off the resolution as the film will register the slightest tremor. These shakes will even be more noticeable if you are using a telephoto and the subject is far away. The best solution is the heaviest, sturdiest tripod you can carry. That extra stability will give you additional quality and allow you to shoot extra shots that are identical to the first.

There are a few more tricks to limit motion. The most obvious is to use a cable release to shoot the photo. You can also lock the mirror in the "up" position to keep it from jerking the camera. If possible, stick to exposures around 1/30 and 1/60 of a second. These are the smoothest speeds in most cameras and will also lessen camera movement.

Finally, keep the object in the center of the photo. Lenses have their best resolution in the center of the screen and many lose their sharpness the farther you go to the edge. If necessary, shoot more than one picture to allow all parts of the target to be photographed in the center.

The final concern is atmospheric conditions. Unfortunately, there isn't as much you can do about that. Haze and smog can be limited by using filters, but you are adding more glass. The best course of action is to plan to take your shots in the morning when the air is cool. This at least cuts down on distortion caused by heat waves.

Having looked at the limitations of high resolution photography, let's look at the theoretical resolution of a photographic opportunity. In this case, the equation is: Resolution = (distance/ focal length) x resolution diameter. If you are using a film with a low contrast resolution of 100 lines per mm, your resolution diameter is .01mm. You are shooting an object 1000 meters away and you are using a 500mm lens. Your theoretical resolution is: (1,000,000/500) x .01 or 20mm. Your possible resolution is ¾ of an inch! That's close enough to see if your target is paying the bill with cash or a credit card, and possibly whether it's American Express or Visa. Before you start checking out your neighbor's spending habits, remember this is the theoretical limit and you need the best conditions and equipment to achieve this.

Resolution Required for Interpretation Tasks (Meters)

Object	Detection	Recognition	Precise Identification	Description	Technical Information
Missile Site	3.0	1.5	0.6	0.30	0.08
Radar	3.0	0.9	0.3	0.15	0.04
Aircraft	4.5	1.5	0.9	0.15	0.03
Nuclear Weapons	2.4	1.5	0.3	0.03	0.01
Submarines	30.5	6.0	1.5	0.9	0.03
Command Headquarters	3	1.5	0.9	0.15	0.03
Vehicles	1.5	0.6	0.3	0.05	0.03

Source: *IEEE Spectrum*, July 1986

Figure 13-1

Depending on the information required, different objects require different levels of clarity.

Now that you can calculate resolution, you can put this to work in determining what you need in a photographic mission. Since high resolution is hard to acquire, it doesn't make sense to risk the mission by taking the time necessary to make a high resolution photo to discover that a young tank commander left his black book on the turret when all you needed was the number of tanks in the compound. Consequently, you need to match the mission requirements with the type of photography.

As a guide, the table (see Figure 13-1) shows military objects, the mission, and the required resolution in meters. A quick glance shows that only technical intelligence missions require high resolution.

Figure 13-2

This photo shows the V-2 rocket test site at Peenemunde. Resolution is approximately three feet. You can see the rockets (A) and a crane (B).

With this information, the analyst can help tailor a mission. If the photographer is supposed to find surface-to-air missile sites around an air base, the required resolution is only 3 meters. If there is a hill overlooking the base 5 kilometers away and you use film with a resolution of .01mm and a 100mm lens, you know that you will have a resolution of .5 meters. That will be more than enough for your needs. In fact, you can instruct the person going on the mission there is enough flexibility that they can avoid attracting attention by hand holding the camera just as a tourist would.

Figure 13-3

This photo shows the assembly building at Peenemunde (C). You can also see another crane and part of the test site in the left-hand corner.

Pushing the Resolution Limit

Up to now we have dealt with simple resolution. Either you have it or you don't. Obviously that doesn't appeal to you or the superpowers. As we mentioned earlier, computers are used to enhance the photos, but that isn't all. Intelligence services use statistics to manipulate the images to show what may not even appear in a photo. Obviously, this is very difficult, requires a bit of computer time, does have a degree of error, and is difficult to do manually with regular film. The other problem is that those who have developed the mathematical models aren't about to divulge them to the public. Consequently, the following is a theoretical approach to improved resolution I have developed. It may or may not be an approach the superpowers use. It doesn't include the specific models, so I recommend you hire a statistician if you plan on developing this.

Up to now we have been talking about resolution based on the number of lines per mm. Theoretically, the ultimate resolution is the size of the grain of silver halide. In this case we could be talking about .05 micrometers or .0005mm. If we plug that number into the previous equation, we have a theoretical resolution of 5mm with a 100mm lens at 1 kilometer! The problem is that equipment and weather prevent you from achieving that.

However, you can try to attain that resolution if you want to take a large series of photos and want to limit yourself to a small part of the film, say less than a square mm.

The sharpness that prevents this resolution is due to the air and glass that the photons must travel through in order to interact with the grain of film. Since you need four photons to cause a film grain to react, the chances that the light from a small object reflects towards the camera, and avoids the air and glass, is something of a random accident. In other words, the small object may appear on one piece of film, but not on others. This randomness can probably best be described as a Poisson distribution. It would indicate the chances an object of a given size would have of appearing on a piece of film. The smaller the object, the smaller the chance that four photons would arrive to react with the film, and the smaller the number of occurrences in a given population. You can achieve improved resolution with high probabilities if you have the time to shoot the required number of shots. The number of photos would depend on the situation and would have to be calculated beforehand. Be warned, that it may be quite a few.

As complex as this sounds, it is mathematical techniques that the intelligence agencies use to push resolution to the absolute limits. It's of limited use in most fields because of its effort, but that's enough for you to start with if you need it.

Figure 13-4

This photo shows Peenemunde after an air strike. The test site has been destroyed, though the assembly building suffered less damage.

14

Photographic
Interpretation

We now come to the last major chapter and probably the hardest part of photographic intelligence, photo interpretation. Although the superpowers have applied a great deal of technology and money to satellite imagery, automated interpretation is still a dream. Consequently, it still revolves around one interpreter and one photo. With the millions of photos produced by spy satellites and the limited number of interpreters, you can be just as accurate in your analysis as the professionals (provided your photos are good enough).

Over the years, people in this business have wondered what makes a good interpreter and why certain interpreters have been better than others in identifying targets. Like being an artist (or writer), it takes desire and a blend of talents. If you can find the right type of person, the rest is easy. Without that combination of talents, your interpretation will be inaccurate.

The best photo interpreter is one who can blend visual perception with mental awareness, since an analyst must be able to unconsciously evaluate several factors and combine many disciplines together. That means the interpreter should have a well-rounded education, a passing familiarity with most fields of knowledge, and the ability to apply this to photo interpretation. In the case of a photographic interpreter analyzing an industrial complex, he needs to know about most manufacturing techniques, industrial equipment, management techniques, transportation capabilities, energy management, and the sciences. And he must be able to unconsciously draw on each area as he views the photo.

If you are trying to identify good candidates for photo interpretation, some researchers have found a strong correlation between the ability of beginners to search for and identify urban-industrial features in aerial photos and their future success in interpretation. Many such photos are available at the library or from a local aerial photography company.

Equipment

Photographic interpretation requires little equipment. Generally, transparencies are used for analysis because the extra step of producing the print destroys detail that may be critical to the interpreter. Prints can be useful, however, if more than one copy is needed or it is required in the field. Even then, some analysis can be made from the negative at a central location.

Whether you are using transparencies or negatives, you should have a light box to view the film. This may be an inexpensive one bought at the local camera shop or a sophisticated piece of equipment made especially for photo interpretation. If you can't buy one, you can make one with a frosted piece of glass and a bank of fluorescent lights under the glass.

The best way to view your films is with a magnifier or loupe. Again, these range in quality from cheap plastic magnifiers to high quality pieces of ground glass. What you want to buy will depend on what your needs are. Some instruments even have scales that allow you to measure objects on the film. That will be useful later in this chapter.

Those people who need to push the film to its maximum resolution might want to consider a microscope. Again, it would be wise to buy one with a scale in the viewfinder to help analyze the information.

If you are viewing stereo photos, you will need a pocket stereoscope. This device deflects the normal viewing pattern of your eyes and allows you to see depth when you view a pair of stereo photos. You can make a pair if you have two magnifying lenses (2 to 3 power) of the same type. They should be placed in a piece of wood so that the distance between the center of the lenses corresponds to the distance between the center of your eyes. This will allow you to view stereo pictures from 6 to 9 inches away.

There are many other tools that can also be used to interpret photos, but a computer that can digitize a photo can be the most important. This equipment is now in the price range that can make it available to most people. In the hands of an expert, a desktop computer can enhance unclear details in a photograph and manipulate it in such a way that it reveals more detail than the original. You can even overlap two images on the computer in order to reveal more detail than either of the originals.

What to Look For

There are no firm rules on what to look for, but these are some general points to consider.

- *Object Recognition.* Try to identify each object in the photo. Be aware of shapes, sizes, patterns and textures of the objects. After you have identified the object, ask yourself why it is in the picture.
- *Changes.* Has the scene changed from previous photos? If so, why? What could those changes mean?
- *Technical Information.* What technical information can be gathered about the opposition's capabilities from the photo? If you aren't an expert in the technical field, find one.
- *Placement.* Placement often reveals use. Headquarters are often centralized while munitions dumps are isolated. A long distance photo of a cockpit can reveal quite a bit even though the toggles and dials are too far away to recognize. The size and location of the features will often give away their use and may even give insight into tactics.
- *Unusual Items.* U2 pilots found an ICBM base in the Soviet Union because there were several railroad tracks leading nowhere. Find out why something appears out of place.

Aerial Photo Interpretation

Interpretation of aerial photos is the most difficult because they present objects in an unusual manner. For instance, from directly above, a cistern and a smokestack look nearly identical. On the other hand, aerial photos can present the most information. Since the art of photo interpretation is too large a subject for this book and since the techniques of aerial photo interpretation can be applied to other photos, we will only investigate this one aspect of photo interpretation. It's up to you to apply the following methods to other types of photography.

Figure 14-1

*Always look for the unusual or out-of-place. The rail in this photo
is the only sign of the Japanese midget sub pen inside the hill.*

Aerial photography is one of the most popular methods of
gathering information. It not only has military applications, but
civilian ones (many governments use it for property assessment).
Therefore, many colleges have courses on the subject and several
textbooks are available for the interested person. If you need to
pursue this subject extensively, a trip to one of these colleges or
a neighboring used bookstore would be helpful.

Measuring With Displacement

Although we think of an aerial photo as providing us with an
overhead shot, that is partially untrue. The only part of the photo

that is truly an overhead shot is the spot directly underneath the camera. The rest of the shot is oblique. In other words, while an overhead shot of a smokestack makes it appear to be a circle, an oblique shot makes it look like a circle with the body of the stack pointing towards the center of the photo. This is called displacement and is useful in determining the height of an object because the displacement increases the farther you move toward the edge of the photo. Therefore, if you know the center of the photo (where the camera is directly overhead) and you know the altitude of the camera, you can determine the height of a building, smokestack, tree, or storage tank (see Figures 14-2 and 4-3). The formula for determining height is:

Height = (Negative displacement/distance from photo center) x Altitude.

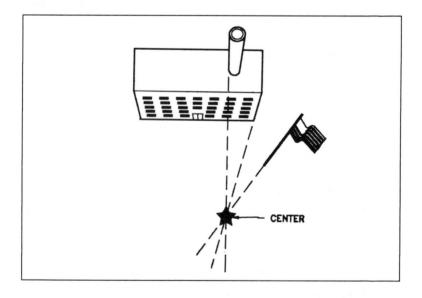

Figure 14-2

The center, or "nadir," of a photo is the point where all vertical lines intersect.

The variables are:

1. Height of the object in feet.

2. The length of the displaced image on the negative in inches.

3. Distance from the center of the photo to the top of the object (in inches).

4. The altitude of the photo when taken (in feet).

Since this equation works on the basis of a relationship, you can use an enlargement or even use metric scale (meters and millimeters). For example, a photo is taken of an industrial site at 4,000 feet. A smokestack measures .2 inch in the print and the top of the smokestack is 3 inches from the center of the picture (the point directly below the camera and closest to the lens). The equation would look like this:

Height = (.2/3) x 4,000 or

Height = .0666 x 4,000 or

Height = 266 feet.

This method is best used with an enlargement or a very accurate scale because a small error can have a very big effect.

Measuring With Shadows

As I mentioned earlier, shadows can be used to measure height. The same applies to determining distance in aerial photos, provided there is a good shadow cast on open ground.

To figure out height by means of shadows, you have to know the angle of the sun. There are three methods for finding sun angle and the object's height. The first is to find an identifiable object of a known height in the photo (such as a phone or electricity line). You can then use the following equation to determine the tangent of the sun's angle:

Sun Tangent = Height of known object/Shadow of object.

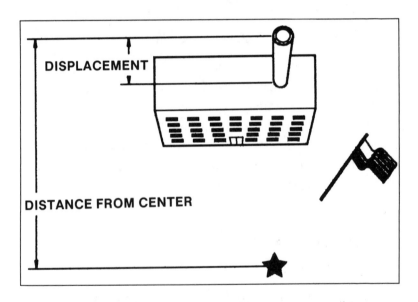

Figure 14-3

The height of an object can be determined from a photograph
if the altitude of the aircraft it was taken from is known.

If a telephone pole is 20 feet high and the shadow cast is 15 feet long, then 20/15 = 1.33. The tangent of the sun's angle is 1.33. This figure can then be applied to other shadows, like the shadow of a smokestack that is 100 feet long. By multiplying the tangent times the shadow length, we know the smokestack is 133 feet high.

If there isn't an object of known height, you can use height and derive the displacement to determine a given height and derive the tangent from that object.

The final method for determining height requires knowing the position of the target and the time the photo was taken. By using astronomical tables and a book on celestial navigation (both available at most boating supply stores) you can determine the angle of the sun at a certain time and day. It's a complicated mathematical process, but it provides an alternative to the other methods.

Calculating Distortions in Photographs

One advantage of aerial photography is that you can photograph objects many miles away. This is particularly useful for identifying objects in a restricted area. The United States uses this technique to spy on hostile countries with the high flying SR 71. The SR 71 flies along the border and uses its sensors to record information on targets hundreds of miles inside the border; all without violating enemy airspace. You can use the same technique, although you can't fly as high as military aircraft. However, even private aircraft can fly high enough to allow someone to photograph something a hundred miles inside enemy territory. Unfortunately, the further the object is away from the camera, the greater the distortion from the earth's curvature and the atmosphere. Like water, the atmosphere bends light waves so that the object appears farther away than it really is. In a highly oblique photograph, the object may be over a mile away from its perceived position.

You can determine the true distance from your aircraft position by recording the aircraft's altitude above land and the angle of the camera when the photo is taken (see Figure 14-4). Be warned that this is a quick and dirty method and errors of up to a hundred feet, at 60 miles, are to be expected. However, a more accurate measurement would require complex calculations and a detailed knowledge of the atmospheric conditions when the photo was taken.

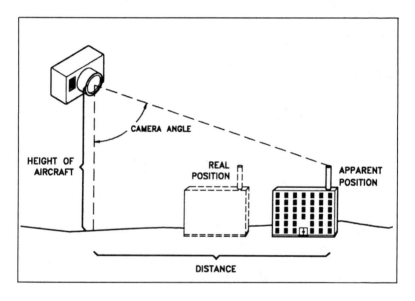

Figure 14-4

You can correct for photographic distortions caused by the atmosphere and the curvature of the earth.

The formula for determining apparent position is:

Distance = (tangent of the camera angle) x height of aircraft over land.

If, for instance, the photograph was taken at 20,000 feet and the camera angle was 60 degrees, then the equation would be: 20,000 x 1.7321 = 34,642 feet away from the point of land the aircraft is directly over.

Of course, this equation assumes the object is the same altitude above sea level that the point under the aircraft is. If it isn't, you have to adjust the altitude figure. For instance, if the target is 1,000 feet above the land under the aircraft, then you subtract 1,000 from the height figure (19,000). If it's 1,000 feet below the level under the aircraft, you add that number (21,000).

You can now correct this first figure for the earth's curvature and atmospheric refraction by using the following formula:

Correction = .574 x (distance in miles, squared).

In the previous equation the correction would be:

Correction = .574 x (6.56 miles squared).

Correction = .574 x (43.04) = 24.7.

Therefore, you would subtract 24.7 feet from the original distance. Admittedly, this isn't much at such a short distance, but it will increase dramatically at long distances. For instance, an object 100 miles away will require a correction of over 1 mile!

Interpreting Agricultural Information

There are many civilian and military reasons for discovering the types of crops grown in an area. Unfortunately, most fields look similar during the winter, spring, and fall. The only time you can identify a crop is when it is mature enough to identify from the air. Mature oats and alfalfa photograph nearly black with panchromatic film. Corn and soybeans are a grey tone, while ripe wheat is usually white. Corn and soybeans may be differentiated by their size (corn is as tall as a man, while soybeans are much smaller) and the size of their shadows.

Another method of identifying a crop is by looking at the type of farming practices. Flooded crops like rice are found in low wavy terraces. Pasture land usually has ponds for the animals and lanes that lead to the barns. Orchards are usually evenly spaced so the trees each have the same amount of space. Vineyards are evenly spaced lines that have more space between them than crops have.

Aerial techniques can also be used to identify the type of trees in a forest. This can help identify the type of soil and climate, be used to determine commercial value, or determine how easily a military unit can pass through it. The easiest method of identifying tree types is comparing the shadows with profiles of common tree types. Since each tree type usually reflects a different cross section of light, the tone of the identified tree can be used in identifying stands of tree types in a forest (especially with panchromatic or infrared film).

The type of terrain can often be determined by studying the drainage patterns — "creekology" as the geologists call it. Flat sedimentary rocks such as sandstone or shale have a dendritic drainage pattern, in other words, a meandering "tree branch" type of pattern. Limestone usually has underground rivers, so they have water filled sinkholes instead of a drainage pattern. Tilted land usually has several parallel streams that drain water from the crest of the ridge. Alluvial land shows the action of rivers like old stream beds, oxbow lakes, and fans from the deposit of material.

Identifying Mines

Most different mining operations can be identified by the geographical features, the method of mining, and the type of processing. Although I can't cover all the types, the following should help you identify major mine types and determine capability.

The best tool for identifying the type of mine is a book on the geography of the area. That should narrow the possible types of material down to a few and may make the choice obvious.

The most important clue to the nature of the mine is the type of extraction: open pit, underground, or drilling. There are others like dredging for gold and platinum, but they aren't major contributors to the mining industry.

Open pit mining is probably the most important technique. It is primarily used in extracting low cost materials or ore deposits close to the surface. The color of the rock can help you detect what it is. For instance, if the rock is black, it is probably coal. If it is a light tone, it may be bauxite, an aluminum ore. If the color changes in the wall of the pit, it means that waste rock covers the ore body. If the ore vein is thin or there is a large amount of waste rock (overburden), the ore is rich or the material being mined is valuable. If there is water at the bottom of the pit, it means the pit is probably a sand or gravel quarry. Open pit mines are the easiest to locate because they cover many acres of ground.

Underground mining is used only for deep, high value, extensive mineral deposits because of the high cost of starting an underground mine. An idea of the mine's size can be gained by the size of the ore cars and signs of underground dewatering (necessary if the mine goes under the water table). With the exception of coal, usually only metals are valuable enough to mine underground. Underground mines are the hardest to find because the opening is small. The best clue for finding a mine is to look for railroad tracks or a road suddenly stopping at the side of a hill. A shaft going underground will have a hoist building surrounding the entrance.

Drilling is usually reserved for oil and gas. Drilling rigs, pipelines, and pumping stations are signs of petroleum extraction. Underground gas or oil lines are visible because vegetation has a hard time regaining a foothold over the pipe. This leaves a straight barren strip of ground as a tell-tale mark.

Most metals aren't refined at the site, but often, enough processing is done there to cut down on transportation. Materials that aren't processed at the mine usually are ones that require extensive processing or other raw materials. Therefore, materials like coal, aluminum ore, or iron ore are often shipped from the mine without processing. Processing plant configurations can often give an idea of the mineral being refined.

One processing method, generally found with open pit mining, is heap leaching. In it, a pile of ore is leveled out and a system of hoses is laid over it to sprinkle a solution over the ore. The solution captures the metal, drains out the bottom of the pile, is collected in a pond, and is stripped in a small processing plant. Heap leaching operations are used in extracting gold, silver, copper, and some uranium ore. This process is only used on low grade ores, never high grade material. The sign of a heap leach is a large pile of crushed ore, several acres in size, leveled flat, and covered with a network of hoses and sprinklers. There are usually a couple of ponds and the processing plant can either be in a semi-trailer (for gold and silver) or a series of three to four large tanks (10 to 15 feet in diameter).

Richer metal ores are usually smelted. This requires a plant with smokestacks and a power source for the heat. Usually piles of the raw material are stacked outside the plant. If the ore is surrounded with a fence, it may be gold or silver ore.

The type and size of the storage facilities can give an idea of the type of ore. Bulky materials like zinc, copper, or lead require warehouses, roads, and transportation facilities that can handle large quantities of material. Certain precious and strategic materials are so portable that they may be stored in a room inside the plant and a transportation facility may not be visible.

Geological information may be important to determining the type of material being mined. If water drainage shows a fault, there may be a mineralized zone that indicates copper, gold, or silver. If drainage shows a dome, then salt, sulfur, or petroleum products may be found in the area. If the mining is occurring in an alluvial plain, heavy materials like gold or titanium may be mined. Unfortunately, there are so many variables that a geologist or a mining engineer may be needed to analyze your information.

Because of their shape, piles of raw materials can be hard to measure. However, if you can determine the height through shadow measurements or the height of other objects, you can make a rough guess of the amount of material in the pile by using the principles of solid geometry. The aerial photo will give the size of the base and top of a pile (plus any other contours). By using the determined height, you can determine the slope of the stockpile and solve the cube much as you would for a cone (the cone volume = (π x cone radius squared x height)/3). The following table gives the weight of certain materials. This may give you an insight into the plant's capability.

Approximate Weights of Material
in Pounds Per Cubic Yard

Cement, portland, loose	2,538
Concrete, 1:2:4 mixture	
trap rock	4,020
gravel	3,945
limestone	3,890
sandstone	3,770
cinder	2,860
Clay, dry, loose	1,700
Clay, damp	2,850
Clay and gravel, dry	2,700
Earth, dry, loose	1,975
Earth, moist, loose	2,110
Earth, moist, packed	2,590
Earth, mud, flowing	2,916
Earth, mud, packed	3,100
Garbage	1,000
Riprap, limestone	2,950
Riprap, shale	2,830
Sand, gravel, dry, loose	2,630
Sand, gravel, dry, packed	2,950
Sand, gravel, wet	3,400
Coal	
Anthracite, natural	2,620
Bituminous, natural	2,270
Lignite, natural	2,110
Anthracite, piled	1,420
Bituminous, piled	1,270

Source: Navstar International

Industrial Identification

Identifying industrial facilities requires a great deal of knowledge of manufacturing processes. Since we can't cover each process (present and future), we will provide some keys to general classifications. These are fabrication, energy dependent processes, and chemical dependent processes.

Figure 14-5

The snow in the aerial photograph of a World War II German aircraft factory hides details and hinders interpretaton.

Fabrication industries make finished goods and are the hardest to identify. Their material usually comes in on rail or truck, so there is some docking facility. Cranes indicate the use of heavy products, while multi-storied buildings mean there is little heavy material being used. Since finished products are usually protected from the weather, identifying the product may mean studying the loading dock, boxes, or the type of transportation. If you need to identify a specific manufacturing facility, a few experts should be brought in and several photos (different angles and different times) should be provided to them. Any information from land-based agents would be helpful.

Energy dependent processes usually transform raw materials through the use of power (usually heat). Power distribution centers or piles of coal are a sign of this activity. Since energy processes often use heat, smokestacks are often evident. Smelters, furnaces, and the manufacture of clay products, aluminum, and cement use this type of process.

Chemical dependent processes use chemicals to manufacture materials. They are identified by the tanks, pipes, and outdoor processing equipment. Very little material handling equipment is evident. Some chemical dependent processes are nitric and sulfuric acid production, petroleum refining, and the manufacture of plastics. Since most explosives are manufactured with chemical processes, special attention should be given to isolated storage sheds where the finished product would be kept.

An idea of the chemical plant's (or refinery's) capability can be made by determining the capacity of the storage tanks. The volume of a cylindrical tank is:

Volume (cu. ft.) = (.7854 x diameter squared) x height.

The cubic feet can be converted into gallons by multiplying by 7.481 or into liters by multiplying by 28.316.

Military Analysis

Identifying a civilian target is difficult. Imagine the problems when someone is trying to hide the information! It takes a skilled eye to notice the deception practiced by an opponent. That is something I can't teach in a few pages. However, I will try to cover some major points about camouflage. If you need specifics, you might want to refer to a book on camouflage and deception.

Figure 14-6

Effective camouflage. The Germans hid this World War II
rocket fuel plant until after the war was over.

Understanding camouflage is similar to understanding a magician's trick. In fact, some of the earliest deception experts were magicians. In order to understand what they are doing, you must understand how camouflage works and how the eye perceives it.

The eye and brain identify an object by recognizing the shape and separating it from the rest of the picture. Camouflage tries to blend the object into the background either by covering it (throwing bushes on top of a tank) or adding a pattern that allows the shape to blend into the background (camouflage painting schemes). Deception, on the other hand, makes decoys stand out from the environment.

Since camouflage and deception can't be perfect, they rely on the observer not to be observant. Consequently, camouflaged planes are designed to fool enemy aircraft for the few seconds it would normally take to attack them. It's also useful against a major power that has so much information gathering capability that its interpreters can't properly evaluate photos. Since the reader will probably have a small intelligence group, you may identify camouflaged objects invisible to the major powers.

The final advantage for the photographic interpreter is that so much of the deception practiced today is directed towards radar and infrared signatures, not visible ones. No better example can be found than the Stealth bomber. It can evade radar and heat seekers, but it is very vulnerable to visual sighting.

Having discussed how camouflage works and some advantages the reader has, let's look at some types of visual camouflage and how they may be countered.

1. *Hiding Targets.* This is the oldest type of camouflage, covering the target with dirt or cut brush. Yet it is one of the most effective because the basic materials are usually available. The weakness, however, is that cut brush, camouflage, or dirt have different reflectance patterns when used in disguises than in a natural position. Consequently, panchromatic film and infrared film can usually identify the hidden target.

Of course, technology has developed camouflage that has infrared signatures closer to real vegetation. However, if you remember, each type of plant has a different pattern, so even a material that has the same reflectance pattern as an oak would still stand out in a grove of maples.

Hidden objects can also be discovered by carefully comparing dimensions and location. What may look like a house may only be the size of a small room (this is a common method of hiding power distribution centers in U.S. suburbs). If an industrial complex is painted to look like a field, an oblique photo will show the difference in height.

2. *Hiding Shape.* The shape of an object is important to identifying an object. If the shape can be broken up with different patterns (as in a camouflage scheme), the eye will often miss it. However, this is generally ineffective against attacking units. A trained interpreter knows that a set of photos taken with different types of film will make the difference stand out. For instance, camouflaged aircraft on a camouflaged field will show dramatic differences with infrared film because the runway will not reflect light the same way vegetation does. In fact, the pattern of stress of grass in the way of the jet blasts will give the interpreter an idea of the way the airfield is used and the type of aircraft that use it (the same with reflectance patterns in the runway itself).

3. *Continuing Natural Patterns.* Troops will often hide equipment in ravines, along hedges, or in some other manner that imitates nature. In addition to different types of film, the interpreter should look for track marks and differences in the road use. For instance, a road that skirts a forest which shows more track patterns on one part of the road than the rest may indicate that the forest is a location for troops and equipment.

The following methods are recommended for identifying camouflage or deception.

1. *Film.* Photograph the scene with at least two types of film (panchromatic and infrared are recommended). Use different

types of filters to block out certain types of light. The photos will probably show the differences that indicate a hidden target.

2. *Camera Angle.* Most camouflage is designed to hide the target from either aerial photography or ground troops. A set of oblique photos will often reveal targets in addition to helping the interpreter identify the height of the object. With the dimensions, an interpreter can also find discrepancies common in camouflaged targets.

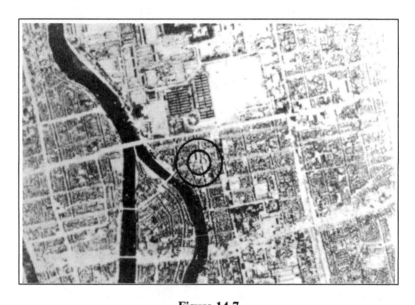

Figure 14-7

Hiroshima before the bomb. Note the fire lanes that criss-cross the city.

3. *Photograph at Different Times.* The change in shadows can often help the interpreter discover a camouflaged item. Since researchers have found shadows are easily noticed by the eye and brain, some countries use this in deception. For instance, the U.S. Air Force has mats that resemble aircraft shadows. The

contrast is so great that pilots recognize them faster than the real aircraft or even a dummy.

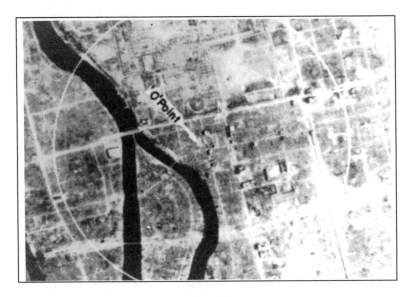

Figure 14-8

Hiroshima after the bomb. Most of the remaining buildings are brick.

4. *Gather Enough Information.* A full set of photos, with different angles, film, and times are the interpreter's best tool. People who have been at the location should also be brought into the process since they will notice irregularities or buildings that have appeared too quickly. Always remember; there is a loophole in camouflage.

One last area that the military interpreter must be familiar with is damage assessment. Specifically, the interpreter must be able to identify the loss of capability, the effort necessary to restore that capability, and how long it will take to regain capability after an attack. That requires knowing the processes involved and the type of repair capability the surrounding area has. A good damage assessment is just as important as any other piece of photo interpretation because it can give a field commander an idea of the enemy's vulnerability.

15

Conclusion

We've come to the end of the book. Some of you may feel that you have learned something while others may feel that most of this is common sense. If you feel that way, you are right. Most of intelligence gathering isn't glamorous spying, but a common sense approach to gathering information that is withheld. Since secrets aren't held in a vacuum, there must be some non-secret manifestation of them. Stealth bombers must be flown outside restricted airspace if they are to be useful and secret manufacturing methods must be incorporated in a factory. This is what real intelligence officers realize and try to find. That's why much of the world's intelligence gathering network is oriented to collecting information from newspapers, technical papers, and regular photos. It is a low risk way to learn something and much of it can be learned in the safety of the home country.

That brings us to the most important part of intelligence, people. The people who work in the world's intelligence agencies are some of the brightest people their country has. Smart, well-trained people aren't wasted in life-threatening missions any more than a queen is used for a gambit in a chess game. The acme of intelligence is to gather what information can be acquired with the minimum of danger, analyze it, and determine the enemy's capabilities and intentions. That is done with common sense and reasoning.

The methods in this book won't make you a world-famous spy. At best your successes will be quiet and limited to knowing a smooth operation was based on information that you provided. And, in the silent world of intelligence, that is high praise indeed.

Appendix I
Foreign
Photographic Restrictions

Most countries have limitations on what you can photograph. Obviously, military installations are sensitive, but photographing civilian installations, such as dams, factories, power plants, bridges, and transportation networks can get you into trouble with the authorities. If you have questions, contact the local embassy. In all cases, use care. Just because it's legal doesn't mean a local authority will not cause trouble. You don't help anybody if you are caught.

The following is a list of some countries and what of a military nature they allow to be photographed (according to various sources). If the appropriate space is blank, it is okay to photograph the site (still, use caution). "Permit" means a permit or official permission is required. "No" means that the subject is extremely sensitive. I've included most countries. Those not included are of minimal military importance. You are on your own there. Remember, this isn't the Bible. Always use caution in taking your shots. Don't expect me to bail you out or raise a rescue mission to get you out of jail.

Country	Military Sites	Civilian Sites	Comments
Albania	no	no	Authorities are sensitive
Algeria	no	no	Acquire photo permit
Angola	no	no	
Argentina	no		
Australia			
Austria	permit		
Belgium	no		
Belize	permit		
Bolivia	permit		
Brazil	permit		
Brunei	no	permit	
Bulgaria	no	no	Authorities are sensitive
Burma	no	no	
Canada	permit		
Chile	no		Be careful about police photos
China (Mainland)	no	no	Authorities are sensitive
China (Taiwan)	permit		
Columbia			
Cuba	no	no	Authorities are sensitive
Cyprus	no	no	

Country	Military Sites	Civilian Sites	Comments
Czechoslovakia	no		Avoid airport photographs
Denmark	permit		
Ecuador	no		Avoid airport photographs
Egypt	no	no	
El Salvador	permit		Some civilian sites may be sensitive
Finland	no	no	
France	no		
Germany (East)	no	no	
Germany (West)	no		Permit possible
Greece	no	no	
Guatemala	no	no	
Haiti	permit		
Honduras	no		
Hong Kong	permit	permit	
Hungary			
India	permit	permit	
Indonesia	no		
Iran	no	no	Authorities are sensitive
Iraq	no	permit	Authorities are sensitive
Ireland	permit		
Israel	no		
Italy	no	no	

Country	Military Sites	Civilian Sites	Comments
Jamaica	permit		
Japan			
Jordan	no	permit	
Kampuchea	no	no	
Kenya	no	permit	
Korea (South)	permit	permit	
Korea (North)	no	no	Authorities are sensitive
Libya	no	permit	
Liberia	no	permit	
Luxembourg	permit		
Malaysia	no	no	
Mexico	no		
Morocco	permit	permit	
Mozambique	no	no	
Namibia	no	no	
Nepal			
Netherlands	no		No railroad shots
New Zealand	permit		
Nicaragua	no	permit	
Norway	no		
Pakistan	no	no	
Panama	no	permit	
Paraguay	no		Get permit
Peru	no	no	
Philippines			
Poland	permit	permit	
Portugal	permit	permit	

Country	Military Sites	Civilian Sites	Comments
Romania	no	no	Authorities are sensitive
Saudi Arabia	no	permit	
Singapore	no	permit	
South Africa	no	no	Authorities are sensitive
Spain	permit	permit	
Sri Lanka	no	permit	
Sweden	no		
Switzerland	no	permit	
Syria	no	no	
Tanzania	no	no	
Thailand	permit	permit	
Trinidad	no	permit	
Tunisia	no	no	
Turkey	no	no	
United Kingdom			
USA			
USSR	no	no	
Uruguay			
Venezuela			
Yugoslavia	no	permit	
Zaire	no	no	
Zimbabwe	no	no	

Appendix II

Sources

I can't include everything you need to know about all the subjects I've talked about. Therefore, I've included a list of books, publications, and societies you can refer to.

AERIAL PHOTOGRAPHY

Photography From Lightplanes and Helicopters, Rochester, NY, Kodak, 1985, Publication No. M-5

Photointerpretation and its Uses, Rochester, NY, Kodak, Publication No. M-42

American Society of Photogrammetry, Falls Church, VA

Remote Sensing and Image Interpretation, Thomas Lillesand and Ralph Keefer, New York, John Wiley & Sons, 1966

COPYING DOCUMENTS

Copying, Rochester, NY, Kodak, 1974, publication No. M-1H

INFRARED PHOTOGRAPHY

Applied Infrared Photography, Rochester, NY, Kodak, 1977, Publication No. M-28

KODAK PUBLICATIONS

Index to Kodak Information, Kodak Publication L-5, Department 454, Eastman Kodak Company, Rochester, NY 14650

PHOTOGRAPHIC INTERPRETATION

The Journal of Strategic Studies, June 1984

Airborne Reconnaissance IX, Proceedings of the Society of Photo-Optical Instrumentation Engineers for 1985, Bellevue, WA

Verification: How Much is Enough?, Stockholm International Peace Research Institute, 1985

Interpretation of Aerial Photography, Minneapolis, MN, Burgess Publishing Co., 1968

SURVEILLANCE

Applied Surveillance Photography, Raymond Siljander, Charles Thomas, Springfield, IL, 1975

Spygame, Scott French and Lee Lapin, CEP Incorporated, Boulder, CO, 1985

Shadowing and Surveillance, Burt Rapp, Loompanics Unlimited, Port Townsend, WA, 1986.

YOU WILL ALSO WANT TO READ: